Anonymous

Allowance of equipment under cognizance of the Bureau of equipment

And recruiting for vessels of the United States Navy. 1890

Anonymous

Allowance of equipment under cognizance of the Bureau of equipment
And recruiting for vessels of the United States Navy. 1890

ISBN/EAN: 9783337723644

Printed in Europe, USA, Canada, Australia, Japan

Cover: Foto ©ninafisch / pixelio.de

More available books at **www.hansebooks.com**

ALLOWANCE OF EQUIPMENT

UNDER COGNIZANCE OF THE

BUREAU OF EQUIPMENT AND RECRUITING

FOR VESSELS OF THE

UNITED STATES NAVY.

1890.

ISSUED BY THE NAVY DEPARTMENT.

WASHINGTON:
GOVERNMENT PRINTING OFFICE.
1890.

NAVY DEPARTMENT,
Washington, January 1, 1890.

The following Allowance of Equipment, under cognizance of the Bureau of Equipment and Recruiting, for vessels of the United States Navy, are approved, and officers of the Navy will be governed thereby.

B. F. TRACY,
Secretary of the Navy.

CONTENTS.

Classification of Vessels for Equipment under cognizance of the Bureau of Equipment and Recruiting.

Name and class.	Displacement.	Rig.
FIRST CLASS.		
Chicago	4,500	Bark.
Philadelphia	4,324	3-masted schooner.
Newark	4,083	Bark.
San Francisco	4,083	3-masted schooner.
....		
....		
....		
....		
....		
....		
....		
....		
SECOND CLASS.		
No sail power.		
Baltimore	4,400	Two military masts.
Charleston	3,730	" " "
....		
....		
....		
....		
....		
....		
THIRD CLASS.		
Lancaster	3,250	Ship.
Brooklyn	3,000	"
Pensacola	3,000	
Hartford	2,900	
Richmond	2,700	
....		
....		
....		
....		

Classification of Vessels for Equipment under cognizance of the Bureau of Equipment, &c.—Continued.

Name and class.	Displacement.	Rig.
FOURTH CLASS.		
Boston	3,000	Brig.
Atlanta	3,000	
No. 7	3,000	Schooner.
Nos. 8	3,000	
FIFTH CLASS.		
Omaha	2,400	Bark.
Galena	1,900	"
Marion	1,900	"
Mohican	1,900	"
Ossipee	1,900	"
Swatara	1,900	"
SIXTH CLASS.		
Iroquois	1,575	Bark.
Kearsarge	1,550	"
Adams	1,375	"
Alliance	1,375	"

Classification of vessels for equipment under cognizance of the Bureau of Equipment, &c.—Continued.

Name and class.	Displacement.	Rig.
SIXTH CLASS—Continued.		
Essex	1,375	Bark.
Enterprise	1,375	"
Nipsic	1,375	"
SEVENTH CLASS.		
No. 9	2,000	Schooner.
No. 10	2,000	"
No. 11 and class	2,000	"
Yorktown	1,703	3-masted schooner.
Concord	1,703	" "
Bennington	1,703	" "
Dolphin	1,485	" "
EIGHTH CLASS.		
Alert	1,020	Bark.
Ranger	1,020	"
Yantic	900	"
Petrel and class	885	Barkentine.
NINTH CLASS.		
Despatch	560	Brigantine.
Nina	420	Schooner.
Mayflower	420	"
Leyden	420	"
Fortune	420	"

Classification of vessels for equipment under cognizance of the Bureau of Equipment, &c.—Continued.

Name and class.	Displacement.	Rig.
NINTH CLASS—Continued.		
Palos	420	Schooner.
Pinta	420	"
Speedwell	420	"
Standish	420	"
Triana	420	"
Triton	70	
IRON-CLADS.		
FIRST CLASS.		
Maine	6,648	3-masted schooner.
Texas	6,300	2 military masts.
Puritan	6,000	1 military mast.
Amphitrite	3,815	1 " "
Miantonomoh	3,815	1 " "
Monadnock	3,815	1 " "
Terror	3,815	1 " "
SECOND CLASS.		
Ajax	2,100	
Camanche	1,875	
Canonicus	2,100	
Catskill	1,875	
Jason	1,875	
Lehigh	1,875	
Mahopac	2,100	
Manhattan	2,100	
Montauk	1,875	

Classification of vessels for equipment under cognizance of the Bureau of Equipment, &c.—Continued.

Name and class.	Displacement.	Rig.
IRON-CLADS—Continued.		
SECOND CLASS—Continued.		
Nahant	1,875	
Nantucket	1,875	
Passaic	1,875	
Wyandotte	2,100	
PADDLE-WHEEL STEAMERS.		
Monocacy	1,370	Schooner.
Tallapoosa	1,270	"
Michigan	685	Barkentine.
SAILING VESSELS.		
Constellation	1,886	Ship.
Portsmouth	1,125	"
Jamestown	1,150	"

NOTE.—Receiving-vessels, hulks, and store-ships will be supplied by the Bureau on special requisitions.

EQUIPMENT.

ANCHORS AND KEDGES.

1. Bower and sheet anchors are to be alike in weight, the weight of an anchor or kedge, *as marked on it*, being inclusive of the bending-shackle and stock.

2. Stream anchors, in all cases, when allowed, are to be about one-fourth the weight of the bower.

3. Kedges, when four are allowed, are to be, respectively, about one-seventh, one-eighth, one-tenth, and one-fourteenth the weight of the bower; when three are allowed, one-sixth, one-eighth, and one-tenth; when two are allowed, one-sixth and one-tenth; and when one is allowed, one-eighth.

4. To determine the weight of a bower or sheet anchor for a vessel, multiply her displacement in tons by the number assigned to her approximate displacement in the following table, in the column headed "Multipliers," and the product will express the number of pounds, *inclusive of stock*.

5. Each boat of every vessel is allowed one anchor; the weight in pounds to be obtained by multiplying the square of the extreme breadth by 1.2.

TABLE I.—*Anchors and kedges.*

Size of vessel.	Multipliers.	Bower.	Sheet.	Stream.	Kedges.
Over 3,700 tons displacement	1¾	2	2	1	4
Over 2,400 tons displacement	2	2	2	1	3
Over 1,900 tons displacement	2¼	2	2	1	3
Over 1,500 tons displacement	2½	2	2	1	3
Over 900 tons displacement	2¾	2	1	1	3
900 tons and under displacement	3	2	1	1	2
Vessels with no sail power	1½	2	1	....	2

Patent or other anchors will be supplied by special order.

EQUIPMENT—Continued.

CHAIN-CABLES, ETC.

Rule to determine the size of chain-cable corresponding to an anchor of a given weight (inclusive of stock).

Cut off the two right-hand figures of the number of pounds of the anchor's weight, and multiply the square root of the remaining quantity by 4; the result will be the diameter of the chain in sixteenths of inches. Thus:

Weight of anchor in pounds 5,000
Cut off two right-hand ciphers, leaves 50
Square root of 50 .... 7.071
$7.071 \times 4 = 28.284$ and $\frac{28}{16} = 1\frac{12}{16}$, the diameter of chain needed.

TABLE II.—*Length of chain-cables.*

Weight of bower-anchor, in pounds, including stock.	Length of chains in fathoms.			Remarks.
	Bower.	Sheet.	Stream.	
Over 7,500	135	135	105	One chain-cable, length and size as indicated by table and rule above, is to go with each bower, sheet, and stream anchor allowed the vessel; except vessels of special types, when special lengths shall be allowed.
Over 5,000	120	120	105	
Over 3,000	120	120	90	
Over 2,000	120	120	90	
Over 1,600	105	105	75	
Over 1,200	90	90	75	
Over 800	90	90	60	
Under 800	60	60	60	

TABLE III.—*Chain-cables for boats.*

When number of boats allowed is—	Length of chain and number allowed.		Remarks.
	Of 30 fathoms.	Of 25 fathoms.	
More than 7	2	2	The size of these chains is to be determined by rule above. If the anchor is of less weight than 100 pounds, take $\frac{1}{10}$ of it for number of sixteenths for chain.
More than 5	1	2	
More than 3	0	2	
Less than 3	0	1	

EQUIPMENT—Continued.

TABLE IV.—*Appendages to chain-cables.*

The articles, as per columns 1, 2, 3, 4, 5, and 6, are to be furnished with each chain-cable a vessel is allowed, to correspond thereto; and those articles in columns 2, 3, 4, 5, and 6 are to be delivered in a suitable box, indorsed with its contents and the size of the cable to which they pertain.

When the size of the cable is—	Chain-hooks.	Cold-chisels.	Punches.	Pins.	Spare shackles.	Keys for shackle-pins.	Spare beading-shackle and club-link.	Mooring-swivels.
Column	1.	2.	3.	4.	5.	6.		
Over 2 inches	20	8	8	12	2	1	One to each vessel.	One for each vessel whose bower chain-cables are of and over $\frac{14}{16}$ of an inch.
Over 1$\frac{11}{16}$ inches	18	6	6	10	2	1		
Over 1$\frac{6}{16}$ inches	16	4	4	8	2	1		
Over 1$\frac{1}{16}$ inches	12	4	4	8	2	1		
Over $\frac{14}{16}$ inch	8	4	4	6	2	1		
Over $\frac{12}{16}$ inch	8	3	3	6	2	1		
Under $\frac{12}{16}$ inch	6	3	3	6	2	1		

NOTE.—Three deck-stoppers for each cable, one bitt-stopper for each bower.

TABLE V.—*Grapnels and iron buoys.*

When the weight of the bower anchor (including stock) is in pounds—	Grapnels.		Grapnels for buoys.		Buoys for anchors.			
	Number.	Weight, in pounds.	Number.	Weight of each, in pounds.	Number.	Height, in inches.	Breadth, in inches.	Weight, in pounds.
Over 7,500	2	140 and 70	2	15	2	44	21	60
Over 5,000	2	100 and 50	2	15	2	44	21	60
Over 3,000	2	80 and 40	2	12	2	44	21	60
Over 2,000	2	60 and 30	2	12	2	44	21	60
Over 1,600	2	50 and 25	2	10	2	30	13$\frac{1}{2}$	30
Over 1,200	2	40 and 20	2	10	2	30	13$\frac{1}{2}$	30
Over 800	2	30 and 15	1	10	2	30	13$\frac{1}{2}$	30
Under 800	1	25	......	......	2	30	13$\frac{1}{2}$	30

EQUIPMENT—Continued.

TABLE VI.—*Stream-cables of manila, hawsers, and tow-lines.*

The number and circumference, in inches, of wire and manilla hawsers and manilla tow-lines, to be furnished to a vessel in the Navy according to the weight of her bower-anchor. Each manilla hawser and tow-line is to be 120 fathoms in length; wire hawsers 100 fathoms in length. All hawsers should be kept on reels, and none stowed in the hold if it can possibly be avoided.

Weight of bower-anchor, including stock.	Hawsers of manila, number allowed having a circumference of—				Tow-lines of manila, number allowed having a circumference of—	Steel-wire hawsers, number allowed having a circumference of—				
Pounds.	6 inches, rope-laid.	7 inches, rope-laid.	8 inches, rope-laid.	9 inches.	5 inches.	3½ inches.	4 inches.	4¼ inches.	4½ inches.	5 inches.
10,000	....	1	1	1	2	....	1	....	1	1
9,500	....	1	1	1	2	....	1	....	1	1
9,000	....	1	1	1	2	....	1	....	1	1
8,500	....	1	1	1	2	....	1	....	1	1
8,000	....	1	1	1	2	1	1	....		
7,500	....	1	1	1	2	1	1	....	1	....
7,000	....	1	1	1	2	1	1	....	1	....
6,500	....	1	1	1	2	1	1	....	1	....
6,000	....	2	1	....	2	1	1	....	1	....
5,500	....	2	1	....	2	1	1	....	1	....
5,000	1	1	1	....	2	1	1	....	1	....
4,500	1	1	1	....	2	1	....	1	....	....
4,000	1	1	1	....	2	1	....	1	....	....
3,500	1	1	....	....	2	1	....	1	....	....
3,000	1	1	....	....	2	1	....	1	....	....
2,500	1	....	....	....	2	1	1	....	....	....
2,000	1	....	....	....	2	1	1	....	....	....

EQUIPMENT—Continued.

VII.—*Table of comparative dimensions of chain-cables, hemp rope, iron and steel rope, their weight per fathom, and breaking-strain.*

Breaking-strain of wire and hemp ropes.	Approximate size of chains corresponding thereto.	Circumference.			Weight per fathom.					Size of wire used in rope (iron and steel.)		Remarks.
		Hemp rope.	Iron-wire rope.	Steel-wire rope.	Chain.	Hemp rope, tarred.	Hemp rope, not tarred.	Iron-wire rope.	Steel-wire rope.	Circumference of rope.	Number of wire.	
Pounds.	Inches.	In.	In.	In.	Pounds.	Pounds.	Pounds.	Pounds.	Pounds.	In.	B. W. G.	
4,880	5/16	2½	1¼	⅞	5.18	1.48	1.25	1.28	----------	1¼	22	Steel and iron wire rope, in accordance with this table, have a hemp heart.
7,040	5/16 full.	3	1½	1 1/16	----------	2.12	1.77	1.72	----------	1½	21	
8,260	⅜ scant.	3⅛	1⅝	1⅛	----------	2.46	1.87	2.12	----------	1⅝	21 full.	
9,580	⅜	3¼	1¾	1¼	7.70	2.66	2.03	2.49	1.29	1¾	20	The sizes of the wire given are those in use at the Government rope-walk at the navy-yard, Boston, Mass.
11,000	⅜ full.	3½	1⅞	1⅜	----------	2.76	2.30	3.06	1.60	1⅞	20 full.	
12,520	7/16	4	2	1½	11.11	3.72	3.09	3.22	1.74	2	19	
14,130	7/16 full.	4½	2⅛	1⅝	----------	4.67	3.89	3.65	2.14	2⅛	19 full.	
18,840	½	4¾	2¼	1¾	14.08	5.69	4.33	4.15	2.51	2¼	18	No data for the weight of steel ropes smaller than 1¼-inch.
19,560	9/16	5¼	2½	1⅞	18.04	6.94	5.29	5.27	3.09	2½	18 full.	
23,660	⅝	5¾	2¾	2	22.20	8.33	6.35	6.31	3.25	2¾	17	Proof-strains to be as nearly as possible one-half the breaking-strain.
28,160	11/16	6½	3	2⅛	25.81	9.66	8.05	7.46	3.68	3	16	
33,050	¾	7¼	3¼	2¼	30.31	12.78	10.09	8.97	4.19	3¼	16 full.	
38,330	¾ full.	7¾	3½	2½	----------	14.35	11.52	10.69	5.32	3½	15	In practice it is advisable to take it at ⅓ of the average breaking-strain.
44,000	13/16	8	3¾	2⅝	37.73	14.65	12.21	12.72	5.97	3¾	14	
50,060	⅞	8½	4	2¾	41.71	16.57	13.80	14.81	6.37	4	14 full.	
56,520	15/16	9	4¼	3⅛	47.81	18.48	15.48	16.71	8.35	4¼	13	
63,360	1	9½	4½	3¼	55.16	20.71	17.25	18.95	9.06	4½	13 full.	
70,880	1 1/16	10¼	4¾	3⅜	66.44	25.83	19.68	21.40	10.02	4¾	12	
78,220	1⅛	11	5	3½	75.27	27.82	23.20	24.20	10.79	5	12 full.	
86,240	1 3/16	11¼	5¼	3¾	83.04	30.57	24.29	27.15	12.84	5¼	11	
94,650	1 3/16 full.	11¾	5½	4	90.40	33.54	26.50	30.52	14.05	5½	11 full.	
103,450	1¼	12¼	5¾	4¼	----------	36.40	28.80	33.95	16.87	5¾	10	
112,640	1 5/16	13½	6	4⅜	102.22	44.17	34.99	37.70	18.10	6	10 full.	
122,220	1⅜	15	6¼	4½	112.27	54.72	43.20	41.65	19.13	6¼		
132,200	1 7/16	15½	6½	4¾	120.84	58.27	46.12	45.90	21.61	6½	9 full.	
142,560	1 7/16 full.	16	6¾	5	130.69	61.84	49.15	52.50	24.44	6¾	8	
153,320	1½	16½	7	5¼	----------	66.03	52.27	56.89	27.42	7	8 full.	

Note.—Column 1 is not a standard of strength of cables. Column 2 is intended to give, as nearly as possible, the size of chains *approximating* in strength to certain given sizes of wire and hemp rope. Weight of wrought-iron per cubic inch = .2816 lb.

EQUIPMENT—Continued.

VIII.—*Data concerning chain-cables, from tests at the Washington navy-yard, during the time of the session of the Wire Board, from iron rolled by the Government, and from iron received under the standard Government test for the same.*

Diameter of chain iron.	Average breaking-strain.	Weight per fathom.
Inches.	Pounds.	Pounds.
¼	4,087	3.35
5/16	6,343*	5.18
⅜	9,300	7.70
7/16	12,620*	11.11
½	16,550	14.08
9/16	21,100*	18.64
⅝	26,100	22.20
11/16	31,600*	25.81
¾	37,580	30.31
13/16	44,130*	37.73
⅞	51,090	41.71
15/16	58,480*	47.81
1	67,000	55.16
1 1/16	71,893	66.44
1⅛	81,000	75.27
1 3/16	89,844	83.64
1¼	110,100	90.10
1 5/16	120,000	102.22
1⅜	124,000	112.27
1 7/16	136,750	120.84
1½	157,750	130.69
1 9/16	164,871	144.59
1⅝	171,600	154.30
1 11/16	177,500	167.16
1¾	217,840	176.98
1 13/16	224,000	189.75
1 15/16	230,874*	223.47
2	255,600	234.48
2⅛	288,548*	263.40
2¼	....	272
2⅜	....	306
2½	....	336

Wire rope, in Table VII, is made at the Boston navy-yard, has a hemp heart, and is laid up right-handed. As an approximate rule, multiplying the square of the circumference of a hemp rope by the decimal .223 for iron wire, and by .12 for steel wire, and extracting the square root of the product, will give the circumference of a wire rope of corresponding strength—that is, a wire rope with a hemp heart; and multiplying the square of the circumference of a hemp-heart wire rope by 4.5 for iron wire, and by 8.4 for steel wire, and extracting the square root of the product, will give at the circumference of a hemp rope of corresponding strength.

* Breaking-strain computed.

EQUIPMENT—Continued.

STANDING AND RUNNING RIGGING.

Length of rigging of all kinds is to be determined by an accurate draft of the vessel to be rigged. For sizes, see tables following.

All standing rigging to be 6-stranded, shroud-laid, galvanized-wire rope; to be wormed, parceled, and served from end to end as a protection against wear and tear, except stays on which sail is carried; to be set up with rigging-screws except topmast rigging, which is to be set up with laniards—upper dead-eyes to be strapped with iron and have a galvanized-iron scored heart (Walton's) at the upper part of the strap. Topmast rigging of fore-and-aft-rigged vessels may be set up on end. Futtock shrouds are to be made of iron rods set up with turn-buckles to the mast, and shackled to top plate.

LOWER RIGGING.

Wire rope for standing rigging is to be thoroughly protected from air and water by painting it with red lead mixed with boiled linseed oil, wormed, parceled with cotton sheeting (which should be painted when on), then served the entire length.

Get the rope on a stretch and measure off the extreme length of each pair of shrouds from the draft. The middle of the length thus determined will be the center of the eye; paint, worm, parcel, paint again, and serve throughout. Then measure off from the center of eye on each leg of a pair of shrouds the required distance, or place, for the eye-seizing. The eye and both legs to two feet below the eye-seizing should be double-served, first parceling with tarred flax, parceling and serving with round-line. Then over this double service, to a distance of one foot below the place marked for the eye-seizing, put on the heading, which consists of tarred flax canvas, marled on with spun-yarn, the marling hitches to be on top. In putting on this heading, commence on each leg below the place marked for the eye-seizing and work towards the center of the eye. When this is done, form the eye and put on the seizing, which is to be covered with tarred flax canvas securely marled on. After the shroud is let down and the eye formed, cut it to the length marked, and so continue until the rigging is all fitted for each mast. The shroud is then ready for turning in. To determine the place for eye-seizings, of No. 1 pair of shrouds, measure off from the center of the eye two and one-half squares of the mast-head on each leg, and mark it for the upper turn of the seizing. The place of seizing for No. 2 to be the same distance, *plus* the diameter of the shroud; for No. 3 the same distance, *plus* twice the diameter, and so on for the others. Both legs of Nos. 1 and 2 will be leathered in the wake of the yard to take the chafe of the lower yards when braced up.

When the rope is first got on a stretch and the first pair of shrouds is measured off, continue the fitting as far beyond the cut-mark (on the legs of the second pair) as the stretch will admit of.

When there is an odd shroud in the fore and main rigging it should be the after shroud; the eye spliced the same length the heading would be, and seized above the crotch of the splice, making the eye the same as if it were a pair of shrouds, and fitted the same as Nos. 3 and 4. If there is an odd shroud in the mizzen rigging it is to be fitted straight (one leg on the starboard and the other on the port side) and spanned with the pendant, forming the mast-head, and should be put over the mast-head first, the same as the pendants are put over the fore or main mast-head.

TOPMAST RIGGING

Is to be fitted in the manner known as "*straight*," with one eye formed out of two pairs of shrouds, which gives two lifts or thicknesses on the mast-head, with four shrouds on each side, making a snug and neat mast-head.

It should be painted, wormed, parceled, painted again, and served the entire length. The shrouds will be double served from center of eye to three or four feet below the futtock-staff. The length of heading from center of eye down to one foot below the eye-seizing is put on the same as the lower rigging. Catharpins are to be of wire rope, wormed, painted, and parceled, and double served throughout; to be fitted with eyes in each end, and should go abaft the mast and seize together in the center.

The topmast-head (Burton) pendants will be wire rope, fitted the same as lower pendants. Each top-mast has four pendants, two forward and two abaft the rigging. The lower ends of pendants to hang six inches below the catharpin-legs.

Pendants to be fitted the same as topmast rigging, without double service, except around their thimbles.

Sword mats will be substituted for double service on the swifters of lower and topmast rigging.

TOPGALLANT RIGGING

Is to be painted, wormed, parceled, painted again, and served the entire length; to go over the funnel on the mast-head. To be fitted in pairs, with eyes formed like the eyes of lower rigging, and seized so as to fit snug over the funnel.

The forward legs to be double served from the center of eye to one foot below the futtock-staff of topmast rigging; the after leg to be double served from center of eye, three feet down; then from a point one foot above cross-trees to one foot below the futtock-staff; both legs to be leathered in the wake of cross-trees, and to set up in the top with dead-eyes.

FORE AND MAIN STAYS.

Are to be fitted separate, with split collars and lashing-eyes, painted, wormed, parceled, painted again, and served the entire length. Double service on ends of fore-stays, commencing from lower part of the end, quarter-seizing around the thimble and up eight feet on the standing parts. *Main stays*, double service around the thimbles, up to lower part of quarter-seizings, on the end and standing parts. The lashing-eyes to be double served before splicing, which does away with outside parceling and hitching.

Collars to be seized together in the loft and leathered down to four feet below the crotch. To be set up with rigging-screws. Lower end of stay to be spliced around thimble where sail is carried.

Chains may be substituted for wire on the main, in the wake of the smoke-stack, when needed.

MIZZEN STAYS.

Single service throughout; collars to be fitted the same as fore and main; double service around the thimble. Lower end to be set up with rigging-screws.

FORE-TOPMAST STAYS

Are to be single; to be set up with rigging-screws; lower end fitted same as lower stay.

MAIN-TOPMAST STAYS.

Fitted the same as the fore-topmast stays; in long ships, with great distances between fore and main masts, they may be brought directly to the deck near the foremast; but in short ships they will pass through chocks between fore trestle-trees, and set up on deck with rigging-screws. Nips to be double served and leathered; collars seized together in the loft.

MIZZEN-TOPMAST STAYS.

Fitted the same as main-topmast stays, and set up in the main-top with three-scored hearts.

FORE-TOPGALLANT STAYS.

Painted, wormed, parceled, painted again, and served the entire length; to be double served on the eyes around the funnels, and from twelve feet above to one foot below the jib-boom; also in the wake of the nip of the clamp on the dolphin-striker, and where they reeve through the bees. All nips to be leathered. Stays to be set up with rigging-screws, lower end spliced around thimble.

MAIN-TOPGALLANT STAYS.

To be fitted the same as the fore, and set up with dead-eyes in the fore-top. To be double served and leathered at the hole in the fore-cap through which they lead; also to be leathered about three feet below the crotch of the eye-splice.

MIZZEN-TOPGALLANT STAYS.

Fitted, served, leathered, and led in the same manner as the main, and set up in the main-top.

FORE AND MAIN TOPMAST BACKSTAYS.

Fitted and measured off the same as the after-shrouds of the fore and main rigging.

MIZZEN-TOPMAST BACKSTAYS

Are fitted with horseshoe eyes.

FORE, MAIN, AND MIZZEN TOPGALLANT BACKSTAYS.

To be painted, wormed, parceled, painted again, and served throughout. Fitted with spliced eyes, which are double served, without outside parceling.

BOAT-DAVIT TOPPING-LIFTS, SPANS, AND GUYS.

To be of wire rope, and served throughout. Spans to which topping-lift pendants are attached to be leathered in the middle. Topping-lifts not to be served.

RULE

For finding the size of the fore and main shrouds, based on the area, in square feet, of the mainsail, topsail, and topgallant sail.

Rankin, in his work, gives a rule for finding the direct pressure of wind, in pounds, on the sails—that is, when it strikes them at right angles, as follows: "Divide the square of the velocity of the wind in knots by 150 for the direct impulse on a flat surface in pounds on the square foot." Assuming the velocity of wind in a storm to be 53 miles per hour, and applying this rule of Rankin, the pressure on the sails will be found to be 19 pounds per square foot of surface. Bracing the lower yards at an angle of 35° with the keel, the wind strikes the sails at an angle of 55°. A simple calculation shows that at this angle the pressure is reduced to 15.6 pounds per square foot. Therefore, multiply the area of these sails by 15.6 and the actual angular force exerted will be the result; and this will be the support in pounds required for the mast. Now find the angle of support, or the angle which the shrouds make with the mast. A convenient method is to take a line from a lower dead-eye abreast the mast and carry it to the center of the mast horizontally, so as to form a right-angle with it, and measure its length in feet. Then measure from this point on the mast the distance to the upper side of the trestle-trees. Now divide the length of the line taken from the dead-eye by the above measurement on the mast, and the result will be the tangent of the angle of support. Then to the log. cosec. of the angle of support add the log. of the angular force, and the result will be the power of support required in pounds *for that angle;* but for greater security add one-half of this amount to it, and the result will be the total power of support desired. Divide the total power of support thus obtained by the number of shrouds proposed for one side; the quotient will be the breaking-strain of a single shroud, which seek in the table of strength for the required size.

In fore and aft rigged vessels, the sail area used in the computation will be that of the mainsail and main gaff-topsail.

This rule involves the same principles as those of Rear-Admiral T. O. Selfridge, adopted and used by him in the preparation of the allowance tables for 1870.

STANDING AND RUNNING RIGGING.

To determine the size of a piece of standing or running rigging.

The size of the fore or main shroud having been determined for hemp, or wire of equivalent strength, from Table VII, use the decimal in the following table corresponding to the rope required by a multiplier. If wire be required, the circumference of the fore or main shroud in iron wire will be the unit used; if hemp or manila, the same circumference in hemp will be the unit, and the product will be the size of the rope required, in terms of the unit employed.

Examples.

Size of fore or main shroud (wire)	5	inches.
Decimal assigned for fore top-mast stay	.90	
For size of stay required	4.50	inches.
Size of fore or main shroud (hemp)	10.75	inches.
Decimal assigned for fore top-sail halliards..........................	.38	
	8600	
	3225	
For size of fore top-sail halliards...........................	4.0850	inches.

Standing and running rigging.

Rigging, etc.	Column of decimals.	Remarks.
Mizzen-pendant or shroud	.74	
Fore or main stay	1.25	
Mizzen stay	.90	
Fore storm-staysail stay	.83	Wire.
Fore or main topmast shroud	.65	
Mizzen-topmast shroud	.54	
Fore-topmast stay	.90	
Main-topmast stay	.88	
Mizzen-topmast stay	.58	
Fore or main topmast backstay	1.00	
Mizzen-topmast backstay	.80	
Fore or main topgallant shroud	.45	
Mizzen-topgallant shroud	.36	
Fore-topgallant stay	.48	
Main-topgallant stay	.53	
Mizzen-topgallant stay	.39	
Fore-topgallant backstay	.69	
Main-topgallant backstay	.69	
Mizzen-topgallant backstay	.48	
Halliards, fore staysail (whip)	.33	
Halliards, fore staysail (pendants)	.45	
Downhauls, fore staysail	.28	
Sheets, fore staysail (whip)	.30	
Sheets, fore staysail (pendants)	.48	
Halliards (whips) fore top-mast staysail	.27	
Downhauls fore top-mast staysail	.28	
Sheet (whips) fore top-mast staysail	.35	
Pendants (sheet) fore top-mast staysail	.50	
Brails fore top-mast staysail	.23	
Net for head-sail		12th hemp.
Halliards fore top-gallant staysail	.31	
Downhauls fore top-gallant staysail	.22	
Whips (sheet) fore top-gallant staysail	.22	
Pendants (sheet) fore top-gallant staysail	.33	
FOREMAST AND YARD.		
Futtock-shrouds	.55	Iron rods set up with turnbuckles.
Slings, standing (jeers and slings combined)	1.10	
Slings, preventer	1.00	Wire.
Lashings for preventer slings	.50	
Pendant tackle-falls	.40	
Jeer-falls	.50	4-strand Manilla.

Manilla rope to be used unless otherwise designated.

Standing and running rigging—Continued.

Rigging, etc.	Column of Decimals.	Remarks.
FOREMAST AND YARD—Continued.		
Jackstays, bending		Iron.
Jackstays, reefing	.33	
Foot-ropes		Wire 2½ inches.
Stirrups		Wire 1¾ inches.
Flemish horses		Wire 1¾ inches.
Lifts	.50	Wire.
Braces	.44	Standing part of wire to extend forward of smoke stack.
Tacks	.57	Four-stranded manilla, tapered to ⅝ size and ⅓ of length on inner end.
Sheets	.50	
Clew-garnets	.35	
Bowlines	.38	
Reef-tackles		Gun tackle purchase.
Buntlines	.30	
Buntline-whips	.28	Fiddle-blocks.
Leech-lines	.24	
Clew-jiggers	.23	
Lift-jiggers	.32	Double and single blocks.
Bunt whips	.30	
Halliards, fore storm-staysail	.36	
Downhauls, fore storm-staysail	.26	
Sheets, fore storm-staysail		Use jiggers.
Swinging-boom topping-lifts	.55	
Swinging-boom topping-lift lizards	.38	
Falls for topping-lifts	.31	
After-guys	.36	
Forward-guys	.36	
Gear tricing-lines	.28	
FORE-TOPMAST AND YARD.		
Catharpin legs	.54	Wire.
Top-burtons	.33	
Runners (jackstays)	.40	Wire.
Top-pendants	.80	Four-strand manilla, long enough to allow mast to land on deck.
Top-tackle falls (two double blocks)	.45	
Jackstays (bending)		Iron.
Jackstays (reefing)	.40	Wire.
Foot-ropes		Wire 2½ inches.
Stirrups		Wire 1¾ inches.
Flemish horses		Wire 1¾ inches.

Manilla rope to be used unless otherwise designated.

Standing and running rigging—Continued.

Rigging, etc.	Column of decimals.	Remarks.
FORE-TOPMAST AND YARD—Continued.		
Parrals	.63	Wire, two parts.
Topsail-tyes (first 5 classes)	.72	Flexible wire.
Topsail-tyes for other classes	.90	Flexible wire, 1 tye.
Halliards for tyes	.38	
Bell's purchase (below 5th class)	.49	
Lifts	.64	Wire.
Braces	.41	
Sheets	.55	Four-strand manilla.
Clew-lines	.40	Two parts.
Bowlines	.34	
Buntlines	.36	
Reef-tackles	.38	Single secret-block on leech of sail.
Clew-jiggers (pendants)	.35	
Clew-jiggers (whips)	.28	
Lift-jiggers	.28	
Bunt-jiggers	.30	Single, or whips.
FORE-TOP-GALLANT-MAST AND YARD.		
Lanyards for shrouds	....	See general rule.
Long mast-ropes	.47	4-strand manilla.
Long yard-ropes	.57	4-strand manilla.
Jackstays	....	Iron.
Foot-ropes	.28	
Stirrups	.24	
Snorters	.24	
Parrals	.32	Wire; to be leathered, double on the bight.
Lifts	.37	Hemp; 4-stranded.
Brace-pendants	.35	Wire.
Whips for brace-pendants	.25	
Halliards	.30	
Sheets	.40	4-strand manilla, tapered.
Clew-lines	.32	
Buntlines	.24	
Lift-jiggers	.23	
Bunt-whips	.23	
Tripping-lines	.24	
Heel-ropes	.28	
MAINMAST AND YARD.		
Futtock-shrouds	.55	Iron rods set up with turnbuckles.
Slings, standing (jeers and slings combined)	1.20	
Slings (preventer)	1.00	Wire.

Manilla rope to be used unless otherwise designated.

Standing and running rigging—Continued.

Rigging, etc.	Column of decimals.	Remarks.
MAINMAST AND YARD—Continued.		
Lashings for slings	.50	
Pendant tackle-falls	.40	
Jeer-falls	.52	4-strand manilla.
Jackstays (bending)		Iron.
Jackstays (reefing)	.33	
Foot-ropes		Wire 2½-inch.
Stirrups		Wire 1¾-inch.
Flemish horses		Wire 1¾-inch.
Lifts	.50	Wire.
Braces	.44	
Tacks	.57	4-strand manilla, tapered to ¾ size and ¼ of length on inner end.
Sheets	.50	4-strand manilla, tapered to ¾ size and ¼ of length on inner end.
Clew-garnets	.35	
Runners for main bowlines	.42	
Whips for bowlines	.25	
Reef-tackles		Gun-tackle purchase.
Buntlines	.30	
Buntline-whips	.28	Shoe-blocks.
Leech lines	.26	
Clew-jiggers	.25	
Lift-jiggers	.32	Double and single blocks.
Bunt-whips	.30	
MAIN-TOPMAST AND YARD.		
Catharpin legs	.54	Wire.
Top-burtons	.35	
Top-pendants	.80	4-strand manilla, long enough to allow mast to land on deck.
Runners (jackstays)	.40	Wire.
Jackstays (bending)		Iron.
Jackstays (reefing)	.40	Wire.
Foot-ropes		Wire 2½-inch.
Stirrups		Wire 1¾-inch.
Flemish horses	.31	Wire 1¾-inch.
Parrals	.68	Wire, two parts.
Preventer-parrals	.50	Wire.
Topsail-tyes (first 5 classes)	.72	Flexible wire.
Topsail-tyes for other classes	.90	Flexible wire.
Halliards for tyes	.38	
Bell's purchase below 5th class	.49	
Lifts	.61	Wire.

Manilla rope to be used unless otherwise designated.

Standing and running rigging—Continued.

Rigging, etc.	Column of decimals.	Remarks.
MAIN-TOPMAST AND YARD—Continued.		
Braces	.42	
Sheets	.58	2 manilla, 4-strand.
Clew-lines	.42	Two parts.
Bowlines	.34	
Buntlines	.36	
Reef-tackles	.40	Single secret-block on leech of sail.
Clew-jiggers (pendants)	.35	
Clew-jiggers (whips)	.28	
Lift-jiggers	.28	
Bunt-jiggers	.30	Single or whip.
Topmast staysail halliards	.32	To be fitted only when required.
Topmast staysail downhauls	.28	
Topmast staysail sheets (pendants)	.51	
Topmast staysail sheets (whips)	.37	
MAIN-TOP-GALLANT-MAST AND YARD.		
Laniards for shrouds	....	See general rule.
Long mast-ropes	.48	4-strand manilla.
Long yard-ropes	.58	
Jackstays	....	Iron.
Foot-ropes	.30	
Stirrups	.24	
Snorters	.24	
Parrals	.34	Wire; leathered, double on bight.
Lifts	.38	4-strand hemp.
Brace-pendants	.36	Wire.
Whips for brace-pendants	.25	
Halliards	.30	
Sheets	.41	4-strand manilla, tapered.
Clew-lines	.34	
Buntlines	.26	
Lift-jiggers	.23	
Bunt-jiggers	.25	
Tripping-lines	.24	
Heel-ropes	.28	
MIZZEN-MAST AND CROSS-JACK YARD.		
Futtock-shrouds	.54	Iron rods, set up with turnbuckles.
Slings	.90	
Pendant tackle-falls	.33	
Foot-ropes	....	Wire 2¼-inch.
Flemish horses	....	Wire 1¾-inch.

Manilla rope to be used unless otherwise designated.

Standing and running rigging—Continued.

Rigging, etc.	Column of decimals.	Remarks.
MIZZEN-MAST AND CROSS-JACK YARD—Cont'd.		
Stirrups		Wire 1¼-inch.
Lifts	.60	Wire.
Braces	.30	
Lift-jiggers	.32	
MIZZEN-TOPMAST AND YARD.		
Laniards for shrouds and stays		See general rule.
Catharpin legs	.40	Wire.
Top-burtons	.30	
Top-pendants	.56	4-strand manilla, long enough to allow the mast to land on deck.
Jackstays (bending)		Iron.
Jackstays (reefing)	.30	Wire.
Foot-ropes		Wire 2½-inch.
Stirrups		Wire 1¼-inch.
Flemish horses		Wire 1¼-inch.
Parrals	.55	Wire, two parts.
Topsail-tyes	.60	Flexible wire.
Bell's purchases	.35	
Lifts	.40	Wire.
Braces	.26	
Sheets	.39	4-strand manilla, tapered, double on board all vessels.
Clew-lines	.32	Two parts.
Bowlines	.26	
Buntlines	.30	
Reef-tackles	.29	Single secret-block on leech of sail.
Clew-jiggers	.28	
Lift-jiggers	.25	
Bunt-jiggers	.24	Single or whip.
MIZZEN-TOP-GALLANT-MAST AND YARD.		
Laniards for shrouds and stays		See general rule.
Long mast-ropes	.35	4-strand manilla, tapered.
Long yard-ropes	.39	4-strand manilla, tapered.
Jackstays		Iron.
Foot-ropes	.26	Hemp.
Stirrups	.21	Hemp.
Parrals	.25	Wire, leathered, double on the bight.
Lifts	.32	Hemp.
Lift-jiggers	.20	
Braces	.23	Single.
Halliards	.26	

Manilla rope to be used unless otherwise designated.

Standing and running rigging—Continued.

Rigging, etc.	Column of decimals.	Remarks.
MIZZEN-TOP-GALLANT-MAST AND YARD—Cont'd.		
Sheets	.31	
Clew-lines	.23	
Buntlines	.20	
Bunt-whips	.18	
Tripping-lines	.20	
Snorters	.20	
Heel-ropes	.20	
STORM-MIZZEN.		
Halliards	.26	Use mizzen-mast whip.
Sheets		Use jiggers.
SPANKER AND GAFF.		
Sheets	.35	
Peak outhaul pendants	.38	
Peak outhaul whips	.26	
Throat pendants	.32	Wire, long enough to reach deck.
Peak pendants	.50	Wire, long enough to reach deck.
Vangs (pendants)	.45	Wire.
Vangs (whips)	.25	
Downhauls	.28	
Clew-ropes	.28	
Upper brails	.19	
Middle brails	.23	
Lower brails	.23	
MAIN-TRYSAIL MAST AND GAFF.		
Peak pendants	.55	Wire, long enough to reach deck.
Throat pendants	.55	Wire, long enough to reach deck.
Vangs (pendants)	.50	Wire.
Vangs (whips)	.25	
Outhaul pendants	.38	
Outhaul whips	.26	
Downhauls	.28	
Clew-ropes	.28	
Tricing-lines	.20	
Upper brails	.19	
Middle brails	.23	
Lower brails	.23	
Sheets	.37	Gun-tackle purchase.
FORE-TRYSAIL MAST AND GAFF.		
Peak pendants	.55	Wire, long enough to reach deck.
Throat pendants	.55	Wire, long enough to reach deck.

Manilla rope to be used unless otherwise designated.

Standing and running rigging—Continued.

Rigging, etc.	Column of decimals.	Remarks.
FORE-TRYSAIL MAST AND GAFF—Continued.		
Outhaul pendants	.38	
Outhaul whips	.26	
Downhauls	.28	
Clew-ropes	.28	
Tricing-lines	.20	
Vangs (pendants)	.50	Wire.
Vangs (whips)	.25	
Upper brails	.19	
Middle brails	.23	
Lower brails	.23	
Sheets	.37	Gun-tackle purchase.
GAFF-TOPSAILS.		
Halliards	.28	Allowed only to vessels with fore and aft rig, and barks.
Downhauls	.28	
Tacks	.30	
Outhauls	.30	
MISCELLANEOUS.		
Awnings, crow-foot halliards	.17	
Awnings, tackles	.21	
Awnings, bull-ropes	.30	
Awnings, earrings		
Awnings, lacings		
Awnings, stops		
Braces (preventer), fore and main yards	.35	One for each yard. Fitted with pendants long enough to reach slings of yard. Falls to be of same length.
Braces (preventer), fore and main-top-sail yards	.35	
Bowlines, windsail		
Conductors, lightning	.15	Copper-wire rope.
Falls, cat	.52	4-strand manilla.
Falls, fish	.44	
Falls for stern-boats	.31	Size graduated by weight of boat.
Falls for quarter-boats	.35	
Falls for waist-boats	.35	4-strand manilla.
Falls for launch	.38	Required when stowed on rail. 4-strand manilla.
Falls, deck-tackles	.44	4-strand manilla.
Falls, stock and bill	.32	
Falls, jigger	.26 & .20	
Falls, compressor (B. D.)	.32	
Fenders, boat		Rope (10 to each launch with laniards).
Fenders, boat		Leather (1 set to all boats but launch with laniards). 10 for double-banked. 8 for single-banked.

Manilla rope to be used unless otherwise designated.

Standing and running rigging—Continued.

Rigging, etc.	Column of decimals.	Remarks.
MISCELLANEOUS—Continued.		
Futtock-staves (iron)		
Gaskets, harbor		1 set for each yard.
Gaskets, sea		1 set for each yard, gaff, and boom.
Guys for fish-davits	.38	Tackles, double and single blocks.
Guys for quarter-davits	.45	Wire.
Guys for waist-davits	.45	Wire.
Gripes for boom-boats and boats stowed on rail	.56	Clamp to gunwales, and set up with turnbuckles.
Gripes, outside boats		Sword-mat gripes.
Girtlines, hammock		2½ manilla.
Hawse-pendants, clear, with shackle	.90	5 fathoms to be chain.
Hawse-ropes	.51	6 fathoms to be chain, sister-hooks.
Hooks, Jacob's ladders		1 set to each vessel.
Halliards, windsail	.14	
Halliards, signal		White rope, braided, one set.
Hooks, fish (for anchors)		Fitted with link and shackle.
Hammocks (lashing)		15-thread manilla.
Hammock-cloth stops		6-thread hamboline.
Hammock jackstays	.31	4-strand hemp, fitted on a bight.
Ladders, Jacob's, lower rigging		Wire 1¾-inch.
Ladders, stern		Wire 1¾-inch.
Ladders, boom		Wire 1¾-inch.
Ladders, fore and main topgallant masts		Wire 1¾-inch.
Ladders, mizzen topgallant mast		Wire 1¾-inch.
Ladders, trysails		Wire 1¾-inch.
Lines, clothes, 2½-inch manila		Fitted with 3-inch jackstay, main and mizzen rigging.
Lines, tricing, for clothes, main and mizzen rigging		Use mast-whips.
Lines, tricing, for hammocks		Use burtons or clew-jiggers.
Mats, chafing		As needed.
Mast-whips	.28	
Ropes, buoy	.60	
Ropes, back, for cat	.25	
Ropes, back, for fish	.23	
Ropes, ridge, for awnings		Wire 1½-inch.
Ropes, foot, for awnings		Wire 1½-inch.
Ropes, grab	.35	Galvanized wire.
Ropes, man, side	.30	Wormed, covered with canvas, and painted.
Ropes, man, hatchways		Assorted, covered with canvas, and painted.
Ropes, hook	.25	

Manilla rope to be used unless otherwise designated.

Standing and running rigging—Continued.

Rigging, etc.	Column of decimals.	Remarks.
MISCELLANEOUS—Continued.		
Rudder pendants and chains	.68	Chains, iron; a short iron tiller should be bolted to after part of rudder. Fitted only when required.
Spans, quarter and waist davits	.15	Wire.
Spans (coal-bag)		4-inch rope for all classes; hemp.
Shank-painters, fitted with triggers	.70	Chain, tapered on inboard end.
Straps, selvagees and others		Assorted.
Stoppers, cat-head, with triggers	.75	Chain, tapered on inboard end.
Stoppers, fighting	.30	Fitted with dead-eyes, rope strapped, with tails coach-whip fashion.
Stoppers, boat		Same size as falls.
Stoppers, bit	.80	Wire.
Stoppers, deck	.56	Wire.
Stoppers, braces, sheets, etc.		Assorted.
Stays, triatic (pendants)	.77	Allowed to vessels carrying boats in-board only; wire.
Stays, storm-mizzen	.60	Wire.
Stays, triatic (span)	.56	Wire.
Swabs, deck		
Swinging-boom pendants	.45	Wire.
Swabs, hand		
Scotchmen, fair leaders (Walton's)		Assorted; enough for equipment.
Scotchmen, others		As many as required.
Sheer-poles, lower rigging		As required; iron.
Sheer-poles, topmast rigging		As required; iron.
Tackles, relieving	.31	Manila. Fitted when required.
Tackles, fore, pendant		Fitted with double blocks.
Tackles, main, pendant		Fitted with double blocks.
Tackles, fore triatic-stay	.42	Fitted with double blocks.
Tackles, main triatic-stay	.42	Fitted with double blocks.
Tackle-pendants, fore-yard	.77	Wire; fitted with lizard.
Tackle-pendants, main-yard	.77	Wire; fitted with lizard.
Tackles, or jiggers for main braces	.20	On standing part of main braces.
Travelers, main-topsail braces		On mizzen-topmast.
Travelers, topsail halliards		One for each fly-block.
Topping-lifts, quarter-davits		Wire.
Topping-lifts, spans		Wire.
Topping-lifts, falls		
Tricing-lines, main braces		
Wheel-ropes	.46	Manilla or wire.

Manilla rope to be used unless otherwise designated.

Standing and running rigging—Continued.

Rigging, etc.	Column of decimals.	Remarks.
MISCELLANEOUS—Continued.		
Wheel-ropes (spare)	.46	Manilla.
Whips, yard and stay, water, pendants	.50	Wire. Lower one of chain with hooks at lower ends, and rings near the lower blocks for connecting the purchases.
Whips, yard and stay, water, falls	.33	Single blocks.
Whips, fore and main yards and stays	.33	Single.
Whips, hatch	.33	

Table of miscellaneous rigging, etc.

[In column Kind, W. denotes iron wire; H. denotes hemp; M. manilla; Ch. chain;

Miscellaneous Rigging, etc.	First Class.			Second Class.			Third Class.			Fourth Class.			Fifth Class.			Sixth Class.			Seventh Class.		
	Chicago, Philadelphia, Newark, San Francisco, and Class.			Baltimore, Charleston.			Brooklyn, Hartford, Lancaster, Pensacola, Richmond.			Boston, Atlanta, No. 7, No. 8, and Class.			Galena, Marion, Mohican, Ossipee, Swatara, Omaha.			Iroquois, Kearsarge, Adams, Alliance, Essex, Enterprise, Nipsic.			Yorktown, Concord, Bennington, No. 8, No. 10, No. 11, and Class.		
	No.	Size.	Kind.	No.	Size.	Kind.	No.	Size.	Kind.	No.	Size.	Kind.	No.	Size.	Kind.	No.	Size.	Kind.	No.	Size.	Kind.
Awning crowfoot halliards		1¾	M.		1½	M.	5	1½	M.		1½	M.	6	1½	M.	5	1¼	M.		1¼	M.
Awning tackles (fore and aft)		2¼	M.		2	M.	5	2	M.		2	M.	5	2	M.	5	2	M		2	M.
Awning bull ropes		3¼	M.		2¾	M.	4	2¾	M.		2¾	M.	4	2½	M.	4	2½	M.		2½	M.
Awning earings		18th	M.		18th	M.	14	18th	M.		15th	M.	14	15th	M.	14	15th	M.		15th	M.
Awning stops		15th	M.		15th	M.		15th	M.		15th	M.		15th	M.		15th	M.		15th	M.
Awning lacings		12th	M.		12th	M.	8	12th	M.		12th	M.	8	12th	M.	6	12th	M.		12th	M.
Bowlines, windsail		15th	M.		15th	M.		15th	M.		15th	M.		15th	M.		15th	M.		15th	M.
Braces, preventer, fore and main yards.	4	3¼	M.				4	3¼	M.				4	3¼	M.	4	3	M.			
Braces, preventer, fore and main-topsail yards.	4	3¼	M.				4	3¼	M.				4	3¼	M.	4	3	M.			
Conductors, lightning																					
Fenders, boat																					
Fenders, boat																					
Falls, cat	1	4¾	M.	1	4½	M.	1	4½	M.	1	4¼	M.	1	4¾	M.	1	3¾	M.	1	4¼	M.
Falls, fish	1	4¾	M.	1	4	M.	1	4½	M.	1	4¾	M.	1	4¾	M.	1	3¾	M.	1	4¼	M.
Falls, stern-boats (a)	2	3¼	M.	2	2¾	M.	2	2¾	M.	2	2¾	M.	2	2¾	M.	2	2½	M.	2	2½	M.
Falls, quarter-boats		3¼	M.		3¼	M.		3¼	M.		3¼	M.		3¼	M.		3¼	M.		3¼	M.
Falls, waist-boats		3¾	M.		3½	M.		3½	M.		3¼	M.		3½	M.		3¼	M.		3¼	M.
Falls for launches		4	M.		4	M.		4	M.		4	M.		4	M.		3¾	M.		3¾	M.
Falls, deck-tackle	1	4½	M.	1	4	M.	1	4	M.	1	4	M.	1	3¾	M.	1	3¼	M.	1	3½	M.
Falls, B D compressors		3½	M.		3	M.		3	M.		3	M.		2¾	M.		2½	M.		2½	M.
Falls, jigger	8	2¾ to 2¼	M.	8	2½ to 1¾	M.	8	2¼ to 1¾	M.	8	2¼ to 1¾	M.	8	2¼ to 1¾	M.	8	2 to 1½	M.	4	2 to 1½	M.
Gaskets, sea (one set for each yard, gaff, and boom).																					
Gaskets, harbor																					
Girtlines, hammock jackstays		2¾	H.		2¾	H.		2¾	H.		2¾	H.		2¾	H.		2½	H.		2½	H.
Girtlines, hammock	6	2¾	M.	6	2½	M.	6	2¾	M.	6	2¾	M.	6	2¼	M.	6	2½	M.	6	2½	M.
Gripes, outside boats																					

Falls for launches in and out tackles, 3-inch manilla, to be fitted when required.

(a) The size of boats' falls given will be modified by the weight of the boats.

Table of miscellaneous rigging, etc.

C. R. copper rope; I. & C. iron and chain. In column Size, Th. denotes thread.]

Eighth Class.			Ninth Class.			Sailing Vessels.			Paddle-wheel Steamers.			Ironclads. First Class.			Ironclads. Second Class.			Remarks.
Alert, Ranger, Yantic, Petrel, and Class.			Fortune, Leyden, Mayflower, Nina, Palos, Pinta, Speedwell, Standish, Triana, Intrepid, Alarm, Despatch, Vesuvius.			Constellation, Portsmouth, Jamestown.			Monocacy, Talapoosa, Michigan.			Amphitrite, Dictator, Miantonomoh, Monadnock, Puritan, Roanoke, Terror, Maine, Texas.			Ajax, Comanche, Catskill, Canonicus, Jason, Lehigh, Mahopac, Manhattan, Montauk, Nahant, Nantucket, Passaic, Wyandotte.			
No.	Size.	Kind.	No.	Size.	Kind.	No.	Size.	Kind.	No.	Size.	Kind.	No.	Size.	Kind.	No.	Size.	Kind.	
5	1¼	M.	3	1	M.	4	1¼	M.	4	1¼	M.	—	—	—	—	—	—	
5	2	M.	3	1¼	M.	4	2	M.	4	2	M.	4	2	M.	4	2	M.	
4	2¼	M.	3	2	M.	4	2½	M.	3	2¼	M.	3	2¼	M.	3	2½	M.	
14	15th	M.	8	12th	M.	14	15th	M.	12	15th	M.	8	15th	M.	8	15th	M.	As many as required.
—	15th	M.	—	12th	M.	—	15th	M.	—	12th	M.	—	15th	M.	—	15th	M.	
8	12th	M.	4	12th	M.	8	12th	M.	6	12th	M.	6	12th	M.	6	12th	M.	
—	15th	M.	—	15th	M.	—	15th	M.	—	15th	M.	—	15th	M.	—	15th	M.	
4	2¾	M.	—	—	—	4	3¼	M.	—	—	—	—	—	—	—	—	—	
4	2¾	M.	—	—	—	4	3¼	M.	—	—	—	—	—	—	—	—	—	
—	—	—	—	—	—	—	—	—	—	—	—	—	—	—	—	—	—	One for each mast. C. R.
—	—	—	—	—	—	—	—	—	—	—	—	—	—	—	—	—	—	Rope, one set, with laniards, to each sailing launch.
—	—	—	—	—	—	—	—	—	—	—	—	—	—	—	—	—	—	Leather, one set, with laniards, to all boats except launches; 16 for double banked; 8 for single banked.
1	3¾	M.	1	3	M.	1	4¼	M.	1	3¾	M.	1	4½	M.	1	3½	M.	To be fitted only when required.
1	3¾	M.	1	3	M.	1	4¼	M.	1	3¾	M.	1	4½	M.	1	3½	M.	
2	3	M.	—	—	—	2	3¼	M.	—	—	—	—	—	—	—	—	—	Size to be determined by weight of boat in special cases.
—	3	M.	—	2¼	M.	—	3	M.	—	3	M.	—	3¼	M.	—	3	M.	
—	3¼	M.	—	—	—	—	3¼	M.	—	3¼	M.	—	3¼	M.	—	3	M.	
—	3½	M.	—	—	—	—	4	M.	—	—	—	—	—	—	—	—	—	Two to each launch when stowed on rail.
1	3½	M.	1	2¾	M.	1	4	M.	1	3½	M.	1	4	M.	1	3½	M.	
—	2½	M.	—	2	M.	—	2½	M.	—	2¼	M.	—	2¾	M.	—	2½	M.	2 to each compressor, and only fitted when required.
6	2 to 1½	M	2	1¼	M.	8	2 to 1½	M.	6	1½ to 1¾	M.	6	2¼ to 1¾	M.	6	2 to 1½	M.	
—	—	—	—	—	—	—	—	—	—	—	—	—	—	—	—	—	—	
—	—	—	—	—	—	—	—	—	—	—	—	—	—	—	—	—	—	One set for each yard; sword mat.
—	2½	H.	—	2½	H.	—	2½	H.	—	2½	4	—	a	—	—	a	—	One pair for each mast.
6	2½	M.	—	—	—	6	2½	M.	—	2½	M.	—	a	—	—	a	—	
—	—	—	—	—	—	—	—	—	—	—	—	—	—	—	—	—	—	Sword-mats fitted with two legs, with thimbles and laniards in ends and with chain and pelican hook in bights.

(a) For monitors, to be fitted as required.

Table of miscellaneous rigging, etc.—Continued.

[In column Kind, W. denotes iron wire; H. denotes hemp; M. manilla; Ch. chain;

Miscellaneous rigging, etc.	First Class.			Second Class.			Third Class.			Fourth Class.			Fifth Class.			Sixth Class.			Seventh Class.		
	Chicago, Philadelphia, Newark, San Francisco, and Class.			Baltimore, Charleston.			Brooklyn, Hartford, Lancaster, Pensacola, Richmond.			Boston, Atlanta, No. 7, No. 8, and Class.			Galena, Marion, Mohican, Ossipee, Quinnebaug, Swatara, Omaha.			Iroquois, Kearsarge, Adams, Alliance, Essex, Enterprise, Nipsic.			Yorktown, Concord, Bennington, No. 9, No. 10, No. 11, and Class.		
	No.	Size.	Kind.	No.	Size.	Kind.	No.	Size.	Kind.	No.	Size.	Kind.	No.	Size.	Kind.	No.	Size.	Kind.	No.	Size.	Kind.
Gripes, inside boats		----	----		----	----		----	----		----	----		----	----		----	----		----	----
Guys, fish-davits	2	3½	M.	2	3½	M.	2	3½	M.	2	3½	M.	2	3¼	M.	2	3	M.	2	3	M.
Guys, quarter-davits	----	2¼	W.	----	2	W.	----	2	W.	----	2	W.	----	2	W.	----	2	W.	----	1¾	W.
Guys, waist-davits	----	2¼	W.	----	2	W.	----	2	W.	----	2	W.	----	2	W.	----	2	W.	----	1¾	W.
Hawse pendants (clear)	1	3¼ 1	W. ch.	1	2¾ 15/16	W. ch.	1	2¾ 15/16	W. ch.	1	2¾ 15/16	W. ch.	1	2½ 15/16	W. ch.	1	2½ 15/16	W. ch.	1	2½ 15/16	W. ch.
Hawse ropes	1	2 15/16	W. ch.	1	1¾ 7/8	W. ch.	1	1¾ 7/8	W. ch.	1	1¾ 7/8	W. ch.	1	1¾ 7/8	W. ch.	1	1½ 7/8	W. ch.	1	1½ 7/8	W. ch.
Hanks (iron, galvanized)																					
Hooks, Jacob's ladders, seized on rigging.																					
Hooks, fish, for anchor	2	----	----	2	----	----	2	----	----	2	----	----	2	----	----	2	----	----	2	----	----
Halliards, signal	--	9 to 12th	H.	--	9 to 12th	H.	--	9 to 12th	H.	--	9 to 12th	H.	--	6 to 9th	H.	--	6 to 9th	H.	--	6 to 9th	H.
Halliards, windsail	----	1½	M.	----	1¼	M.	----	1¼	M.	----	1¼	M.	----	1¼	M.	----	1¼	M.	----	1¼	M.
Hammock-cloth, stops	----	6th	H.	----	6th	H.	----	6th	H.	----	6th	H.	----	6th	H.	----	6th	H.	----	6th	H.
Ladders, Jacob's, lower rigging (a)																					
Ladders, rope, stern																					
Ladders, rope, boom																					
Ladders, rope, topgallant-mast, fore and main.																					
Ladders, rope, topgallant-masts, mizzen.																					
Ladders, trysails																					
Lines, clothes (short)	----	2¼	M.	----	2¼	M.	----	2¼	M.	--	2¼	M.	----	2¼	M.	----	2¼	M.	----	2¼	M.
Lines, tricing																					
Mats for chafing-gear																					
Mast-whips	----	2½	M.	----	2½	M.	----	2½	M.	----	2½	M.	----	2½	M.	----	2¼	M.	----	2¼	M.
Relieving-tackles	----	3	M.	----	3	M.	----	3	M.	----	3	M.	----	3	M.	----	2¾	M.	----	2¾	M.
Ratlines																					

(a) Wire rope to be set up with turnbuckles.

Table of miscellaneous rigging, etc.—Continued.

C. R. copper rope; I & C. iron and chain. In column Size, Th. denotes thread.]

Eighth Class.			Ninth Class.			Sailing Vessels.			Paddle-wheel Steamers.			Ironclads. First Class.			Ironclads. Second Class.			Remarks.
Alert, Ranger, Yantic, Petrel, and Clue.			Fortune, Leyden, Mayflower, Nina, Palos, Pinta, Speedwell, Standish, Triana, Intrepid, Alarm, Despatch, Vesuvius.			Constellation, Portsmouth, Jamestown.			Monocacy, Talapoosa, Michigan.			Amphitrite, Dictator, Miantonomoh, Monadnock, Puritan, Roanoke, Terror, Maine, Texas.			Ajax, Camanche, Catskill, Canonicus, Jason, Lehigh, Mahopac, Manhattan, Montauk, Nahant, Nantucket, Passaic, Wyandotte.			
No.	Size.	Kind.	No.	Size.	Kind.	No.	Size.	Kind.	No.	Size.	Kind.	No.	Size.	Kind.	No.	Size.	Kind.	
																		As many as required.
2	3	M.	2	2½	M.	2	3	M.	2	2¾	M.	2	3¼	M.	2	3	M.	Tackles; double and single blocks.
	1¾	W.		1¾	W.		2	W.		2	W.		2¼	W.		1¾	W.	Two to each boat.
	1¾	W.					2	W.		2	W.		2¾	W.		1¾	W.	Two to each boat.
1	2¼ 11/16	W. ch.				1	2¾ 11/16	W. ch.	1	2¼ 11/16	W. ch.	1	3¼ 11/16	W. ch.	1	2¼ 11/16	W. ch.	5 fathoms to be chain, with shackle.
1	1½ 7/16	W. ch.	1	3¼ 5/16	H. ch.	1	1¾ 7/16	W. ch.	1	1¼ 7/16	W. ch.	1	2 7/8	W. ch.	1	1½ 7/8	W. ch.	Sister-hooks, 6 fathoms to be chain.
																		As many as required; Lowe's patent.
																		One set to each vessel.
2			1			2			1			1			1			Fitted with link and shackle, and made to correspond to anchor.
	6 to 9th	H.		6 to 9th	H.		6 to 9th	H.		6 to 9th	H.		6 to 9th	H.		6 to 9th	H.	White rope, braided; one set.
	1¼	M.		1¼	M.		1¼	M.		1¼	M.		1¼	M.		1¼	M.	As many as required.
	6th	H.					6th	H.		6th	H.							Hambroline, one set.
																		As many as required. Wire 1¾ inches.
2¼	M.						2¼	M.										Fitted with 3-inch jackstays, main and mizzen rigging, one set.
																		Use mast-whips.
																		As needed.
	2¼	M.		1¾	M.		2¼	M.		2	M.		2½	M.		2¼	M.	Two for each mast.
	2¾	M.					2¾	M.		2½	M.		3	M.		2¾	M.	As required.
																		Iron, sufficient to go in the wake of the doublings of the lower rigging.

Table of miscellaneous rigging, etc.—Continued.

[In column Kind, W. denotes iron wire; H. denotes hemp; M. manilla; Ch. chain;

Miscellaneous, Rigging, etc.	First Class.			Second Class.			Third Class.			Fourth Class.			Fifth Class.			Sixth Class.			Seventh Class.		
	Chicago, Philadelphia, Newark, San Francisco, and Class.			Baltimore, Charleston.			Brooklyn, Hartford, Lancaster, Pensacola, Richmond.			Boston, Atlanta, No. 7, No. 8, and Class.			Galena, Juniata, Marion, Mohican, Ossipee, Quinnebaug, Swatara, Omaha.			Iroquois, Kearsarge, Adams, Alliance, Essex, Enterprise, Nipsic.			Yorktown, Concord, Bennington, No. 9, No. 10, No. 11, and Class.		
	No.	Size.	Kind.	No.	Size.	Kind.	No.	Size.	Kind.	No.	Size.	Kind.	No.	Size.	Kind.	No.	Size.	Kind.	No.	Size.	Kind.
Ratlines, standing rigging. (a)	--	21 & 18th	H.	--	21 & 18th	H.	--	21 & 18th	H.	--	21 & 15th	H.	--	21 & 15th	H.	--	21 & 15th	H.	--	& 15th	H.
Ropes, buoy	2	6½	M.	2	5½	M.	2	5½	M.	2	5½	M.	2	5	M.	2	4¾	M.	2	4¾	M.
Ropes, back, for cat	2	2¾	M.	2	2¼	M.	2	2¼	M.	2	2¼	M.	2	2¼	M.	2	2	M.	2	2	M.
Ropes, back, for fish	2	2½	M.	2	2¼	M.	2	2	M.	2	2	M.	2	2	M.	2	1¾	M.	2	1¾	M.
Ropes, ridge, for awnings																					
Ropes, grab																					
Ropes, man, side (b)	----	2½	M.	----	2½	M.	----	2½	M.	----	2½	M.	----	2½	M.	----	2½	M.	----	2½	M.
Ropes, man, hatchways. (b)																					
Ropes, hook	4	2¾	M.	4	2¾	M.	4	2½	M.	4	2½	M.	4	2½	M.	4	2½	M.	4	2½	M.
Rigging for boats*																					
Rungs for Jacob's ladders																					
Spans, quarter and waist-davits	----	2	W.	----	2	W.	----	2	W.	----	2	W.	----	2	W.	----	2	W.	----	2	W.
Scotchmen, fairleaders (Walton's)																					
Scotchmen, other																					
Shank-painters, fitted with triggers (c).	4	7/16	Ch.	4	[illegible]	Ch.	4	[illegible]	Ch.	4	[illegible]	Ch.	4	[illegible]	Ch.	4	[illegible]	Ch.	2	[illegible]	Ch.
Straps,	48	----	M.	48	----	M.	48	----	M.	48	----	M.	48	----	M.	48	----	M.	48	----	M.
Stoppers, cathead, fitted with triggers (a).	4	7/16	Ch.	4	[illegible]	Ch.	4	[illegible]	Ch.	4	[illegible]	Ch.	4	[illegible]	Ch.	4	[illegible]	Ch.	2	[illegible]	Ch.
Stoppers, fighting	10	3¼	H.	----	----	----	30	2¾	H.	10	2¾	H.	30	2½	H.	30	2½	H.	10	2¼	H.
Stoppers, boats'																					
Stoppers, bitt	2	3¾	W.	2	3¾	W.	2	3¾	W.	2	3¾	W.	2	3¾	W.	2	3¾	W.	2	3½	W.
Stoppers, deck, wire, with lanyards	12	4	W.	12	4	W.	12	4	W.	12	4	W.	12	4	W.	12	4	W.	0	3	W.
Stoppers, braces, sheets, etc.																					
Stays, triatic (span)	1	2½	W.	----	----	----	1	2½	W.	1	2½	W.	1	2¼	W.	1	2	H.	----	----	----
Stays, triatic (pendants)	2	3	W.	----	----	----	2	3	W.	2	3	W.	2	2¾	W.	2	2½	W.	----	----	----
Swabs, deck	48	----	----	48	----	----	48	----	----	36	----	----	30	----	----	36	----	----	30	----	----
Swabs, hand	48	----	----	48	----	----	48	----	----	48	----	----	24	----	----	24	----	----	48	----	----
Sheer-poles, lower rigging	----	----	I.	----	----	----	----	----	I.	----	----	I.	----	----	I.	----	----	I.	----	----	I.
Sheer-poles, topmast rigging	----	----	I.	----	----	----	----	----	I.	----	----	I.	----	----	I.	----	----	I.	----	----	I.

*Steam-launches to be rigged with two lugs; other launches, sloop-rigged with jib; cutters and whale-boats, sliding-gunter fashion with one sprit-sail, without jib.

(a) Enough for equipment.

Table of miscellaneous rigging, etc.—Continued.

C. R. copper rope; I. & C. iron and chain. In column Size, Th. denotes thread.]

Eighth Class.			Ninth Class.			Sailing Vessels.			Paddle wheel Steamers.			Ironclads. First Class.			Ironclads. Second Class.			Remarks.
Alert, Ranger, Yantic, Petrel, and Class.			Fortune, Leyden, Mayflower, Nina, Palos, Pinta, Speedwell, Standish, Triana, Intrepid, Alarm, Despatch, Vesuvius.			Constellation, Portsmouth, Jamestown.			Monocacy, Tallapoosa, Michigan.			Amphitrite, Dictator, Miantonomoh, Monadnock, Puritan, Roanoke, Terror, Maine, Texas.			Ajax, Camanche, Catskill, Canonicus, Jason, Lehigh, Mahopac, Manhattan, Montauk, Nahant, Nantucket, Passaic, Wyandotte.			
No.	Size.	Kind.	No.	Size.	Kind.	No.	Size.	Kind.	No.	Size.	Kind.	No.	Size.	Kind.	No.	Size.	Kind.	
	16 & 15th	H.		15th	H.		21 & 15th	H.		15th	H.							
2	4¾	M.				2	4¾	M.	2	4¼	M.	2	5	M.	2	4¾	M.	
2	2	M.				2	2	M.	2	1¾	M.							
2	1¾	M.				2	1¾	M.	2	1¾	M.							
																		One set, fitted to set up with turnbuckles. Wire 1½ inches.
																		One set, galvanized wire covered with canvas and painted white.
	2½	M.		2	M.		2½	M.		2½	M.		2½	M.		2¼	M.	As required.
																		Assorted as required.
4	2½	M.	2	1½	M.	4	2½	M.	4	2½	M.	4	2½	M.	4	2½	M.	
																		As required.
																		Enough for equipment.
	2	W.		1¾	W.		3	W.		2	W.		2	W.		2	W.	As required for boats.
																		Assorted, enough for equipment.
																		Assorted, enough for equipment.
2	$\frac{5}{16}$	Ch.	2	$\frac{5}{16}$	Ch.	4	$\frac{7}{16}$	Ch.	2	$\frac{5}{16}$	Ch.	2	$\frac{7}{16}$	Ch.	2	$\frac{5}{16}$	Ch.	Galvanized-iron chains, inboard end tapered.
48		M.	12		M.	48		M.	24		M.	16		M.	18		M.	Assorted.
2	$\frac{5}{16}$	Ch.	2	$\frac{5}{16}$	Ch.	4	$\frac{7}{16}$	Ch.	2	$\frac{5}{16}$	Ch.	2	$\frac{7}{16}$	Ch.	2	$\frac{5}{16}$	Ch.	Galvanized-iron chains, inboard end tapered.
24	2¼	H.				30	2½	H.	12	2¼	H.							Fitted with dead-eyes, rope strapped with tails, coach-whip fashion.
																		Same size as falls; two to each boat.
2	2¼	W.				6	3½	W.										
0	3	W.	6	2½	W.	12	3¾	W.	6	3½	W.	6	4	W.	6	3¾	W.	
																		Assorted as needed.
						1	2½	W.										Allowed only to vessels carrying boats inboard.
						2	3	W.										Allowed only to vessels carrying boats inboard.
30			6			36			24			24			24			
24			12			24			18			24			24			
		I.			I.			I.			I.							As many as required.
		I.						I.										

out jibs or jiggers; commanding officers' gigs, two sprit-sails and jibs, or sliding-gunter fashion without jib, at the option of the commander; dinghys,

(b) To be wormed, covered with canvas, and painted.

(c) In vessels with sheet-anchors stowed in waist, only two allowed.

Table of miscellaneous rigging, etc.—Continued.

[In column Kind, W. denotes iron wire; H. denotes hemp; M. manilla; Ch. chain;

Miscellaneous Rigging, etc.	First Class.			Second Class.			Third Class.			Fourth Class.			Fifth Class.			Sixth Class.			Seventh Class.		
	Chicago, Philadelphia, Newark, San Francisco, and Class.			Baltimore, Charleston.			Brooklyn, Hartford, Lancaster, Pensacola, Richmond.			Boston, Atlanta, No. 7, No. 8, and Class.			Galena, Marion, Mohican, Ossipee, Swatara, Omaha.			Iroquois, Kearsarge, Adams, Alliance, Essex, Enterprise, Nipsic.			Yorktown, Concord, Bennington, No. 9, No. 10, No. 11, and Class.		
	No.	Size.	Kind.	No.	Size.	Kind.	No.	Size.	Kind.	No.	Size.	Kind.	No.	Size.	Kind.	No.	Size.	Kind.	No.	Size.	Kind.
Swinging-boom pendants	4	1¾	W.	4	1¾	W.	4	1¾	W.	4	1¾	W.	4	1¾	W.	4	1¾	W.	4	1¾	W.
Tackles, fore-pendant		3¾	W.		3½			3½	M.		3½	M.		3¼	M.		3¼	M.		3¼	M.
Tackles, main-pendant		3¾	M.		3½			3½	M.		3½	M.		3¼	M.		3¼	M.		3¼	M.
Tackles, fore-stay, triatic	1	3¾	M.				1	3½	M.	1	3½	M.	1	3½	M.	1	3¼	M.			
Tackles, main-stay, triatic	1	3¾	M.				1	3½	M.	1	3½	M.	1	3½	M.	1	3¾	M.			
Tackle-pendants, fore yard	1	3	W.	1	3	W.	1	3	W.	1	3	W.	1	2¾	W.	1	2½	W.			
Tackle-pendants, main yard	1	3	W.	1	3	W.	1	3	W.	1	3	W.	1	2¾	W.	1	2½	W.			
Tackles or jiggers for main braces	2	2¼	M.	2	1¾	M.	2	1¾	M.	2	1¾	M.	2	1¾	M.	2	1½	M.			
Turnbuckles, Jacob's ladders (brass)																					
Travelers main-topsail braces																					
Travelers topsail halliards																					
Topping-lifts, quarter-davits		2	W.		2	W.		2	W.		2	W.		2	W.		2	W.		2	W.
Topping-lifts, spans		2¼	W.		2¼	W.		2¼	W.		2¼	W.		2¼	W.		2¼	W.		2¼	W.
Topping-lifts, falls		2¾	M.		2½	M.		2¼	M.		2¼	M.		2¼	M.		2	M.		2	M.
Tricing-lines, main braces	2	21th	H.	2	21th	H.	2	21th	H.	2	21th	H.	2	21th	H.	2	18th	H.			
Whips, yard and stay, water, pendants.	4	2¼	W.				4	2	W.	4	2	W.	4	2	W.	4	1¾				
Whips, yard and stay, water, falls	2	3½	M.				2	3	M.	2	3	M.	2	2¾	M.	2	2¾	M.			
Whips, fore and main yards, and stays	4	3½	M.				4	3	M.	4	3	M.	4	2¾	M.	4	2¾	M.			
Wheel-ropes (sets)	3	5	M.	3	4¼	M.	3	4¼	M.	3	4¼	M.	3	4	M.	3	3¾	M.	3	3¾	M.
Whips, hatch	5	3½	M.	5	3	M.	3	3	M.	5	3	M.	3	2¾	M.	3	2¾	M.	3	2¾	M.
Tackles, sail, fore-topsail																					
Tackles, sail, main-topsail																					
Tackles, sail, mizzen-topsail																					

Note.—Boarding, splinter, and torpedo nettings are only furnished in time of war, and then as required by commanding officer.

Table of miscellaneous rigging, etc.—Continued.

C. R. copper rope; I. & C. iron and chain; Hd. bble. In column Size, Th. denotes thread.)

Eighth Class.			Ninth Class.			Sailing Vessels.			Paddle-wheel Steamers.			Ironclads. First Class.			Ironclads. Second Class.			Remarks.
Alert, Ranger, Yantic, Petrel, and Class.			Fortune, Leyden, Mayflower, Nina, Palos, Pinta, Speedwell, Standish, Triana. Intrepid. Alarm, Despatch, Vesuvius.			Constellation, Portsmouth, Jamestown.			Monocacy, Talapoosa, Michigan.			Amphitrite, Dictator, Miantonomah, Monadnock, Puritan, Roanoke, Terror, Maine, Texas.			Ajax, Camanche, Catskill, Canonicus, Jason, Lehigh, Mahopac, Manhattan, Montauk, Nahant, Nantucket, Passaic, Wyandotte.			
No.	Size.	Kind.	No.	Size.	Kind.	No.	Size.	Kind.	No.	Size.	Kind.	No.	Size.	Kind.	No.	Size.	Kind.	
4	1¾	W.	----	----	----	4	1¾	W.	1	1¾	W.	----	----	----	----	----	----	
----	3	M.	----	----	----	----	3¼	M.	----	3	M.	----	----	----	----	----	----	Fitted with double blocks. Two to each mast.
----	3	M.	----	----	----	----	3¼	M.	----	3	----	----	----	----	----	----	----	
----	----	----	----	----	----	1	3¾	M.	----	----	----	----	----	----	----	----	----	Fitted with double blocks. Allowed only to vessels carrying boats inboard.
----	----	----	----	----	----	1	3¼	M.	----	----	----	----	----	----	----	----	----	
----	----	----	----	----	----	1	3	W.	----	----	----	----	----	----	----	----	----	Fitted with lizards.
----	----	----	----	----	----	----	3	W.	----	----	----	----	----	----	----	----	----	Fitted with lizards.
2	1½	M.	----	----	----	2	1½	M.	----	----	----	----	----	----	----	----	----	On standing part of main braces.
----	----	----	----	----	----	----	----	----	----	----	----	----	----	----	----	----	----	As required for Jacob's ladders, etc.
----	----	----	----	----	----	----	----	----	----	----	----	----	----	----	----	----	----	On mizzen topmast.
----	----	----	----	----	----	----	----	----	----	----	----	----	----	----	----	----	----	One for each fly-block.
----	2	W.	----	----	----	----	2	W.	----	1¾	W.	----	----	----	----	----	----	As many as required.
----	2¼	W.	----	----	----	----	2¼	W.	----	2	W.	----	----	----	----	----	----	
----	2	M.	----	----	----	----	2	M.	----	1¾	M.	----	----	----	----	----	----	
2	16th	H.	----	----	----	2	18th	H.	----	----	----	----	----	----	----	----	----	Fitted with short pendants and thimble.
4	1½	W.	----	----	----	4	1¾	W.	----	----	----	----	----	----	----	----	----	Lower one of chain with hooks at lower ends, and rings near the lower blocks for connecting the purchases.
2	2½	M.	----	----	----	2	2¾	M.	----	----	----	----	----	----	----	----	----	Single blocks.
4	2½	M.	----	----	----	4	2¾	M.	----	----	----	----	----	----	----	----	----	Single.
3	3½	M.	2	3	M.	3	3¾	M.	2	3¼	M.	3	4	M.	3	3½	M.	One set to be of flexible iron wire. Fitted as required.
3	2½	M.	2	2¼	M.	3	2¾	M.	3	2½	M.	4	2¾	M.	3	2½	M.	
----	----	----	----	----	----	----	----	----	----	----	----	----	----	----	----	----	----	Use top-burtons.
----	----	----	----	----	----	----	----	----	----	----	----	----	----	----	----	----	----	Use top-burtons.
----	----	----	----	----	----	----	----	----	----	----	----	----	----	----	----	----	----	Use top-burtons.

BOATSWAIN'S DEPARTMENT.

Articles furnished by Bureau of Equipment to the rigging lofts at naval stations to rig a vessel. These articles should be required from estimates made out as exactly as possible.

Strapping, ratline, etc.	Strapping, ratline, etc.
*Blades, hacksaw	Red lead .... pounds.
Boiled linseed-oil .... gallons.	Ratline, 21-thread .... fathoms.
Canvas, old .... yards.	Ratline, 18-thread .... fathoms.
Canvas, No .... bolts.	Ratline, 15-thread .... fathoms.
Cotton sheeting, unbleached .... yards.	Seizing-stuff, ¼-inch wire .... pounds.
Duck, Raven's .... bolts.	Seizing-stuff, ⅜-inch wire .... pounds.
*Hand-saw files	Seizing-stuff, ½-inch wire .... pounds.
Houseline .... pounds.	Seizing-stuff, $\frac{3}{8}$-inch wire .... pounds.
Hambroline .... pounds.	Tacks, copper .... papers.
Leather .... sides.	Tar .... barrels.
Marline .... pounds.	Tallow .... pound
Needles, sail, assorted	Twine .... pounds.
Oil of tar .... barrels.	Worming, soft .... pounds.
Palms, mounted	Roundline, 4-yarn .... pounds.
*Pincers (flat mouth)	Yarn, spun, 3-yarn .... pounds.
*Pincers (round mouth)	Yarn, spun, 2-yarn .... pounds.

* As many as necessary to fit wire rigging.

BOATSWAIN'S DEPARTMENT—Continued.

[In column Kind, H denotes hemp ;

Articles.	First Class.		Second Class.		Third Class.		Fourth Class.		Fifth Class.		Sixth Class.		Seventh Class.	
	Chicago, Philadelphia, Newark, San Francisco, and Class.		Baltimore, Charleston.		Brooklyn, Hartford, Lancaster, Pensacola, Richmond.		Boston, Atlanta, No. 7, No. 8, and Class.		Galena, Marion, Mohican, Ossipee, Swatara, Omaha.		Iroquois, Kearsarge, Adams, Alliance, Essex, Enterprise, Nipsic.		Yorktown, Concord, Bennington, No. 9, No. 10, No. 11, and Class.	
	1 year.	Kind.	1 year.	Kind.	1 year.	Kind.	1 year.	Kind.	1 year.	Kind.	1 year.	Kind.	1 year.	Kind.
Axes, junk	2	-----	2	-----	2	-----	2	-----	2	-----	1	-----	1	-----
Brushes, clamp	24	-----	24	-----	24	-----	18	-----	18	-----	12	-----	12	-----
Brushes, colr (a)	144	-----	144	-----	144	-----	100	-----	100	-----	100	-----	84	-----
Brushes, hand	60	-----	60	-----	60	-----	48	-----	48	-----	36	-----	36	-----
Brushes, tar, long-handled	10	-----	10	-----	10	-----	6	-----	6	-----	4	-----	4	-----
Brushes, tar, short-handled	5	-----	5	-----	5	-----	4	-----	4	-----	2	-----	2	-----
Brooms, corn	144	-----	144	-----	144	-----	100	-----	100	-----	84	-----	84	-----
Commanders	1	-----	1	-----	1	-----	1	-----	1	-----	1	-----	1	-----
Conductors (lightning)	1	C. R.	1	C. R.	1	C. R.	1	C. R.	1	C. R.	1	C. R.	1	C. R.
Calls, silver (b)														
Cordage, 6-thread, seizing ... pounds	150	H.	100	H.	150	H.	150	H.	150	H.	100	H.	100	H.
Cordage, 9-thread, seizing ... do	150	H.	100	H.	150	H.	150	H.	150	H.	100	H.	100	H.
Cordage, 12-thread ... do	50	M.	50	M.	68	M.	50	M.	68	M.	68	M.	30	M.
Cordage, 12-thread, seizing ... do	75	M.	75	H.	140	H.	75	H.	140	H.	100	H.	50	H.
Cordage, 15-thread, ratline ... fathoms	200	H.	100	H.	200	H.	200	H.	100	H.	100	H.	100	H.
Cordage, 18-thread ... do	50	M.	50	M.	100	M.	50	M.	100	M.	100	M.	50	M.
Cordage, 18-thread, ratline ... do	200	H.	100	H.	400	H.	200	H.	200	H.	200	H.	300	H
Cordage, 21-thread, ratline ... do	400	H.	100	H.	400	H.	400	H.	400	H.	400	H.	-----	-----
Cordage, 24-thread, ratline ... do	200	H.	100	H.	200	H.	200	H.	200	-----	-----	-----	-----	-----
Cordage, 1½-inch ... do	100	M.	75	M.	100	M.	75	M.	50	M.	75	M.	50	M.
Cordage, 1¾-inch ... do	100	M.	50	M.	150	M.	100	M.	75	M.	125	M.	150	M.
Cordage, 2-inch ... do	100	M.	50	M.	150	M.	100	M.	300	M.	250	M.	100	M.
Cordage, 2¼-inch ... do	200	M.	-----	-----	300	M.	300	M.	225	M.	200	M.	-----	-----
Cordage, 2½-inch ... do	150	M.	100	M.	250	M.	175	M.	200	M.	175	M.	150	M.
Cordage, 2¾-inch ... do	100	M.	50	M.	150	M.	150	M.	125	M.	100	M.	50	M.
Cordage, 3-inch ... fathoms	150	M.	25	M.	150	M.	100	M.	125	M.	40	M.	40	M.
Cordage, 3¼-inch ... do	100	M.	50	M.	150	M.	125	M.	150	M.	75	M.	75	M.
Cordage, 3½-inch ... do	100	M.	120	M.	150	M.	100	M.	100	M.	50	M.	50	M.
Cordage, 3¾-inch ... do	125	M.	100	M.	50	M.	50	M.	50	M.	-----	-----	-----	-----
Cordage, 4-inch ... do	100	M.	50	M.	50	M.	50	M.	50	M.	60	M.	60	M.
Cordage, 4¼-inch ... do	100	M.	-----	-----	50	M.	30	M.	30	M.	-----	-----	-----	-----
Cordage, 4½-inch ... do	50	M.	50	M.	50	M.	50	M.	-----	-----	-----	-----	-----	-----
Cordage, 5-inch ... do	-----	-----	-----	-----	-----	-----	-----	-----	-----	-----	-----	-----	-----	-----

(a) The brush back to be of hard wood. The cover to be secured to the brush by six (6) brass screws. The hole to be bored through covering well into back of brush. Tufts number 7 one way by 17 the other, are 1½ inches long, and ¼ inch diameter at base.

(b) One for each boatswain's mate allowed, and two spare ones additional.

BOATSWAIN'S DEPARTMENT—Continued.

M. manilla; C. R. copper rope.]

Eighth Class.		Ninth Class.		Sailing Vessels.		Paddle-wheel Steamers.		Ironclads. First Class.		Ironclads. Second Class.		Remarks.
Alert, Ranger, Yantic, Petrel, and Class.		Fortune, Leyden, Mayflower, Nina, Palos, Pinta, Speedwell, Standish, Triana, Intrepid, Alarm, Despatch, Vesuvius.		Constellation, Portsmouth, Jamestown.		Monocacy, Tallapoosa, Michigan.		Amphitrite, Dictator, Miantonomoh, Monadnock, Puritan, Roanoke, Terror, Maine, Texas.		Ajax, Comanche, Catskill, Canonicus, Jason, Lehigh, Mahopac, Manhattan, Montauk, Nahant, Nantucket, Passaic, Wyandotte.		
1 year.	Kind.	1 year.	Kind.	1 year.	Kind.	1 year.	Kind.	1 year.	Kind.	1 year.	Kind.	
1				1								
12		6		12		6		24		12		
72		24		120		48		144		84		
36		12		36		18		24		24		
4		1		4		1		4				
2		2		2		2		4		4		
72		18		84		36		144		60		
1				1								
1	C. R.			1	C. R.	1	C. R.					
75	H.	20	H.	100	H.	20	H.	20	H.	20	H.	
75	H.	20	H.	100	H.	20	H.	20	H.	20	H.	
68	M.	25	M.	68	M.	68	M.	68	M.	68	M.	
70	H.	15	H.	100	H.	15	H.	15	H.	15	H.	
100	H.			200	H.	100	H.	100	H.	100	H.	
100	M.	25	M.	100	M.	100	M.	100	M.	100	M.	
300	H.	50	H.	300	H.	50	H.	100	H.	100	H.	
				400	H.							
50	M.	50	M.	75	M.	100	M.					
120	M.	60	M.	125	M.	75	M.			25	M.	
250	M.	25	M.	250	M.	75	M.	25	M.	20	M.	
150	M.	40	M.	200	M.	25	M.			30	M.	
100	M.			175	M.	75	M.	40	M.	25	M.	
60	M.			100	M.			25	M.			
40	M.			100	M.			40	M.	40	M.	
40	M.			100	M.			100	M.	50	M.	
		20	M.	50	M.			100	M.			
60	M.					20	M.			30	M.	
				60	M.			100	M.	20	M.	
								100	M.			
								50	M.			

NOTE.—The allowances of stores for the several classes of vessels herein named shall be for one year, and those quantities only shall be put on board at the commencement of a cruise; but as certain articles are required for constant consumption, and others seldom or not at all required, the additional stores allowed for any subsequent year of cruise shall not exceed those allowed for the first year. Should any stores remain over at the expiration of any year of the cruise, they shall be regarded as a part of the allowance for the ensuing year, and no articles not absolutely required for use shall be obtained from naval storekeepers or purchased abroad.

BOATSWAIN'S DEPARTMENT—Continued.

[In column Kind, H. denotes hemp.

Articles.	First Class. Chicago, Philadelphia, Newark, San Francisco, and Class.		Second Class. Baltimore, Charleston.		Third Class. Brooklyn, Hartford, Lancaster, Pensacola, Richmond.		Fourth Class. Boston, Atlanta, No. 7, No. 8, and Class.		Fifth Class. Galena, Juniata, Marion, Mohican, Ossipee, Quinnebaug, Swatara, Omaha.		Sixth Class. Iroquois, Kearsarge, Adams, Alliance, Essex, Enterprise, Nipsic.		Seventh Class. Yorktown, Concord, Bennington, No. 9, No. 10, No. 11, and Class.	
	1 year.	Kind.	1 year.	Kind.	1 year.	Kind.	1 year.	Kind.	1 year.	Kind.	1 year.	Kind.	1 year.	Kind.
Cordage, 5½-inch .... do	----	----	----	----	----	----	----	----	----	----	----	----	----	----
Cordage, lanyard stuff, 4-stranded .... do	----	----	----	----	----	----	----	----	----	----	----	----	----	----
Cod-line .... pounds	225	H.	225	H.	225	H.	150	H.	150	H.	100	H.	90	H.
Spun-yarn, 2-yarn .... do	150	H.	150	H.	150	H.	125	H.	125	H.	100	H.	80	H.
Spun-yarn, 3-yarn .... do	150	H.	150	H.	150	H.	125	H.	125	H.	100	H.	80	H.
Marline (tarred) .... do	150	H.	100	H.	275	H.	150	H.	200	H.	175	H.	100	H.
Roundline .... pounds	100	H.	50	H.	175	H.	100	H.	150	H.	125	H.	50	H.
Houseline .... do	300	H.	200	H.	300	H.	250	H.	250	H.	200	H.	150	H.
Halliards (signal)	----	----	----	----	----	----	----	----	----	----	----	----	----	----
Fairleaders (Walton's)	18	----	18	----	18	----	18	----	12	----	12	----	12	----
Fids, setting	2	----	2	----	2	----	2	----	2	----	1	----	1	----
Fids, splicing	4	----	4	----	4	----	4	----	4	----	4	----	2	----
Grains	1	----	1	----	1	----	1	----	1	----	1	----	1	----
Grapnels, hand	4	----	4	----	4	----	4	----	3	----	3	----	2	----
Hacksaws, hand (wire rigging)	3	----	3	----	3	----	3	----	3	----	3	----	2	----
Hanks (iron), galvanized	----	----	----	----	----	----	----	----	----	----	----	----	----	----
Hammock lashings	----	----	----	----	----	----	----	----	----	----	----	----	----	----
Hammock-rings (iron)	----	----	----	----	----	----	----	----	----	----	----	----	----	----
Harpoons	1	----	1	----	1	----	1	----	1	----	1	----	1	----
Heavers, hickory	6	----	6	----	6	----	6	----	6	----	4	----	3	----
Hooks, single (assorted)	75	----	75	----	75	----	50	----	50	----	40	----	40	----
Hooks, sister (assorted)	60	----	60	----	60	----	40	----	40	----	30	----	30	----
Hooks, fishing (assorted)	200	----	200	----	200	----	150	----	150	----	125	----	100	----
Hooks, shark	2	----	2	----	2	----	2	----	2	----	2	----	2	----
Hatchets	5	----	5	----	5	----	3	----	3	----	3	----	2	----
Hammers	2	----	2	----	2	----	2	----	2	----	2	----	2	----
Junk .... pounds	500	H.	500	H.	2,000	H.	500	H.	1,200	H.	1,000	H.	200	H.
Jack, or riggers' screws .... sets	2	----	2	----	2	----	2	----	2	----	1	----	1	----
Jackasses (rope)	4	H.	4	H.	4	H.	4	H.	4	H.	4	H.	4	H.
Knives (shoemakers')	3	----	3	----	3	----	3	----	3	----	3	----	2	----
Links, chain (split for steering-quadrant)	10	----	10	----	10	----	10	----	10	----	10	----	6	----
Lines, fishing (assorted)	60	----	60	----	60	----	50	----	50	----	40	----	30	----
Leather, rigging, sides of	4	----	1	----	6	----	3	----	4	----	3	----	3	----

BOATSWAIN'S DEPARTMENT—Continued.

M. manilla.

Eighth Class.		Ninth Class.		Sailing Vessels.		Paddle-wheel Steamers.		Ironclads. First Class.		Ironclads. Second Class.		Remarks.
Alert, Ranger, Yantic, Petrel, and Class.		Fortune, Leyden, Mayflower, Nina, Palos, Pinta, Speedwell, Standish, Triana, Intrepid, Alarm, Despatch, Vesuvius.		Constellation, Portsmouth, Jamestown.		Monocacy, Talapoosa, Michigan.		Amphitrite, Dictator, Miantonomoh, Monadnock, Puritan, Roanoke, Terror, Maine, Texas.		Ajax, Canonicus, Catskill, Comanche, Jason, Lehigh, Mahopac, Manhattan, Montauk, Nahant, Nantucket, Passaic, Wyandotte.		
1 year.	Kind.	1 year.	Kind.	1 year.	Kind.	1 year.	Kind.	1 year.	Kind.	1 year.	Kind.	
-----	-----	-----	-----	-----	-----	-----	-----	-----	-----	-----	-----	
-----	-----	-----	-----	-----	-----	-----	-----	-----	-----	-----	-----	One spare set of laniards in coil for all sizes of standing rigging.
80	H.	10	H.	100	H.	40	H.	225	-----	50	H.	For hammock-clews, to be of 3-thread white hemp.
75	H.	15	H.	100	H.	25	H.	20	H.	20	H.	
75	H.	-----	-----	100	H.	-----	-----	20	H.	20	H.	
125	H.	15	H.	175	H.	25	H.	15	H.	15	H.	
90	H.	10	H.	125	H.	20	H.	20	H.	10	H.	
50	H.	10	H.	200	H.	100	H.	50	H.	10	H.	
-----	-----	-----	-----	-----	-----	-----	-----	-----	-----	-----	-----	One spare set throughout, same size as allowed for equipment.
12	-----	-----	-----	12	-----	12	-----	-----	-----	-----	-----	Assorted.
1	-----	-----	-----	1	-----	-----	-----	-----	-----	-----	-----	
2	-----	1	-----	4	-----	2	-----	2	-----	1	-----	
1	-----	-----	-----	1	-----	-----	-----	-----	-----	-----	-----	
2	-----	-----	-----	2	-----	2	-----	3	-----	2	-----	
2	-----	1	-----	3	-----	1	-----	3	-----	-----	-----	
-----	-----	-----	-----	-----	-----	-----	-----	-----	-----	-----	-----	One-fifth the number required for equipment. Low's.
-----	-----	-----	-----	-----	-----	-----	-----	-----	-----	-----	-----	Two sets—one fitted—one in coil—15th.
-----	-----	-----	-----	-----	-----	-----	-----	-----	-----	-----	-----	Galvanized. One set.
1	-----	-----	-----	1	-----	-----	-----	-----	-----	-----	-----	
2	-----	2	-----	4	-----	4	-----	4	-----	4	-----	
35	-----	12	-----	40	-----	25	-----	12	-----	12	-----	
30	-----	12	-----	30	-----	25	-----	12	-----	12	-----	
100	-----	25	-----	125	-----	50	-----	100	-----	75	-----	
2	-----	-----	-----	-----	-----	-----	-----	1	-----	-----	-----	
2	-----	1	-----	3	-----	1	-----	1	-----	1	-----	
2	-----	1	-----	2	-----	1	-----	2	-----	2	-----	
700	H.	150	H.	1,000	H.	250	H.	200	H.	200	H.	If a greater quantity can be conveniently stored, it may be allowed.
1	-----	-----	-----	1	-----	1	-----	-----	-----	-----	-----	A set to consist of three screws.
4	H.	2	H.	4	H.	2	H.	2	H.	2	H.	
2	-----	1	-----	3	-----	1	-----	1	-----	1	-----	
6	-----	-----	-----	10	-----	4	-----	10	-----	6	-----	Supplied only to vessels having steering-quadrants.
30	-----	10	-----	40	-----	10	-----	40	-----	30	-----	
3	-----	1	-----	3	-----	1	-----	1	-----	1	-----	

BOATSWAIN'S DEPARTMENT—Continued.

[In column Kind, H. denotes hemp;

Articles.	First Class.		Second Class.		Third Class.		Fourth Class.		Fifth Class.		Sixth Class.		Seventh Class.	
	Chicago, Philadelphia, Newark, San Francisco, and Class.		Baltimore, Charleston.		Brooklyn, Hartford, Lancaster, Pensacola, Richmond.		Boston, Atlanta, No. 7, No. 8, and Class.		Galena, Juniata, Marion, Mohican, Ossipee, Quinnebaug, Swatara, Omaha.		Iroquois, Kearsarge, Adams, Alliance, Essex, Enterprise, Nipsic.		Yorktown, Concord, Bennington, No. 9, No. 10, No. 11, and Class.	
	1 year.	Kind.	1 year.	Kind.	1 year.	Kind.	1 year.	Kind.	1 year.	Kind.	1 year.	Kind.	1 year.	Kind.
Leather, bellows, sides of	3	-----	2	-----	6	-----	4	-----	4	-----	3	-----	3	-----
Marline-spikes (assorted sizes)	60	-----	60	-----	60	-----	50	-----	60	-----	40	-----	30	-----
Marline-spikes (steel)	6	-----	6	-----	6	-----	6	-----	6	-----	6	-----	6	-----
Mallets, serving	8	-----	8	-----	8	-----	6	-----	6	-----	5	-----	4	-----
Mauls (iron)	3	-----	3	-----	3	-----	3	-----	3	-----	3	-----	2	-----
Needles, sail	100	-----	100	-----	100	-----	80	-----	80	-----	70	-----	60	-----
Palms, mounted	20	-----	20	-----	20	-----	15	-----	15	-----	12	-----	12	-----
Pincers (flat-mouth) sets	1	-----	1	-----	1	-----	1	-----	1	-----	1	-----	1	-----
Pincers (round-mouth) do	1	-----	1	-----	1	-----	1	-----	1	-----	1	-----	1	-----
Rules, two-foot	1	-----	1	-----	1	-----	1	-----	1	-----	1	-----	1	-----
Seines	1	75-fm.	1	75-fm.	1	60-fm.	1	60.fm.	1	60-fm.	1	60-fm.	1	0-fm.
Seizing, wire	-----	-----	-----	-----	-----	-----	-----	-----	-----	-----	-----	-----	-----	-----
Serving-boards	8	-----	8	-----	8	-----	6	-----	6	-----	5	-----	4	-----
Sand	-----	-----	-----	-----	-----	-----	-----	-----	-----	-----	-----	-----	-----	-----
Tags, Dennison pounds	400	-----	400	-----	400	-----	300	-----	250	-----	250	-----	200	-----
Twine, seine do	15	-----	16	-----	15	-----	10	-----	10	-----	10	-----	10	-----
Twine, sewing (flax) do	40	-----	40	-----	40	-----	30	-----	30	-----	25	-----	25	-----
Thimbles, assorted	60	-----	50	-----	50	-----	50	-----	50	-----	40	-----	40	-----
Tar barrels	2	-----	1	-----	2	-----	2	-----	2	-----	1	-----	1	-----
Tar, coal do	2	-----	2	-----	2	-----	2	-----	2	-----	1	-----	1	-----
Tar, oil of do	1	-----	1	-----	1	-----	1	-----	1	-----	1	-----	1	-----
Tape-line (wire-wove, 100 feet)	1	-----	1	-----	1	-----	1	-----	1	-----	1	-----	1	-----

BOATSWAIN'S DEPARTMENT—Continued.

M. manila; C. R. copper rope.]

Eighth Class.		Ninth Class.		Sailing Vessels.		Paddle-wheel Steamers.		Ironclads. First Class.		Ironclads. Second Class.		Remarks.
Alert, Ranger, Yantic, Petrel, and Class.		Fortune, Leyden, Mayflower, Nina, Palos, Pinta, Speedwell, Standish, Triana, Intrepid, Alarm, Despatch, Vesuvius.		Constellation, Portsmouth, Jamestown.		Monocacy, Talapoosa, Michigan.		Amphitrite, Dictator, Miantonomoh, Monadnock, Puritan, Roanoke, Terror, Maine, Texas.		Ajax, Camanche, Catskill, Canonicus, Jason, Lehigh, Mahopac, Manhattan, Montauk, Nahant, Nantucket, Passaic, Wyandotte.		
1 year.	Kind.	1 year.	Kind.	1 year.	Kind.	1 year.	Kind.	1 year.	Kind.	1 year.	Kind.	
3		1		3		1		1		1		
30		6		40		6		12		12		
6		2		6		2		2		2		For fitting wire rigging.
4		1		5		1		1		1		
2		1		3		1		3		1		
50		12		70		18		20		20		Assorted.
12		4		12		6		6		6		Roping and seaming, assorted.
1				1								A set to be *three* in number, of different sizes, for working wire rigging.
1				1								A set to be *three* in number, of different sizes, for working wire rigging.
1		1		1		1		1		1		
1	40-fm.			1	60-fm.							To be put up in barrels.
												1st, 3d, 4th, 5th, 6th, and 7th classes, 300 fathoms of ½, 5/16, ¼ and 3/16 inch; 2d and 8th classes, 100 fathoms of same.
4		1		5		1		1		1		
												As much as needed.
200				250				200		200		
10				10								
20		5		25		10		10		10		
30		12		40		24		12		12		
1		½		1		½		½		½		
1		½		1		1		1		1		
1		½		1		½		½		½		
1		1		1		1		1		1		

CARPENTER'S DEPARTMENT.

Miscellaneous.	First Class. Chicago, Philadelphia, Newark, San Francisco, and Class.		Second Class. Baltimore, Charleston.		Third Class. Brooklyn, Hartford, Lancaster, Pensacola, Richmond.		Fourth Class. Boston, Atlanta, No. 7, No. 8, and Class.		Fifth Class. Galena, Juniata, Marion, Mohican, Ossipee, Quinnebaug, Swatara, Omaha.		Sixth Class. Iroquois, Kearsarge, Adams, Alliance, Essex, Enterprise, Nipsic.		Seventh Class. Yorktown, Concord, Bennington, No. 9, No. 10, No. 11, and Class.	
	Outfit.	Stores, 1 year.	Outfit.	Stores, 1 year.	Outfit.	Stores, 1 year.	Outfit.	Stores, 1 year.	Outfit.	Stores, 1 year.	Outfit.	Stores, 1 year.	Outfit.	Stores, 1 year.
Awls, brad		10		10		10		8		8		6		6
Apparatus, boat-detaching	2		2		2		2		2		2		2	
Awls, scratch		3		3		3		2		2		2		2
Baskets, coal	150		150		100		150		100		75		100	
Brushes, dusting		3		3		3		2		2		2		2
Bath-bricks		75		75		75		50		50		50		40
Brushes, whitewash		24		24		24		18		18		15		12
Cork jackets														
Candle-stands (tin)		40		35		35		30		30		25		18
Charcoal ... barrels.		4		4		3		3		3		3		2
Coal for steaming														
Coal, bituminous														
Cocks, stop, for starting hose		2		2		2		2		2		1		1
Conductor-points	3	2	3	2	3	2	3	2	3	2	3	2	3	2
Engines, handy-billy	1		1		1		1		1		1		1	
Fire-grenades ... doz.	5		5		5		4		4		4		4	
Hooks and eyes, brass (for furniture)		48		48		48		36		36		36		30
Hose, leading ... feet.														
Hose, force-suction ... feet.	45		45		45		30		36		36		27	
Hose, washers'		100		100		100		80		80		80		70
Hose, main-pump ... sets.					2				1		1			
Hose-pipes, flexible rubber	4	2	4	2	4	2	3	1	3	1	3	1	3	1
Hose-couplings ... sets.		3		3		3		2		2		2		2
Hose-coupling expander	1		1		1		1		1		1		1	
Hose-spanners	6	6	6	6	6	6	5	5	5	5	5	5	4	4
Irons, hand, nickel-plated														
Irons leg, nickel-plated														
Leather, pump ... sides.		2		2		2		2		2		2		2
Lime, slaked ... casks.		10		8		8		8		8		6		6
Paste, polishing ... 1-lb. boxes.		40		40		20		30		20		15		30
Pick-axes and grubbing-hoes		2		2		2		2		2		2		2
Rungs for Jacob's ladders		24		24		24		20		20		15		15

CARPENTER'S DEPARTMENT—Continued.

Eighth Class.		Ninth Class.		Sailing Vessels.		Paddle-wheel Steamers.		Ironclads. First Class.		Ironclads. Second Class.		Remarks.
Alert, Ranger, Yantic, Petrel, and Class.		Fortune, Leyden, Mayflower, Nina, Palos, Pinta, Speedwell, Standish, Triana, Intrepid, Alarm, Despatch, Vesuvius.		Constellation, Portsmouth, Jamestown.		Monocacy, Talapoosa, Michigan.		Amphitrite, Dictator, Miantonomoh, Monadnock, Puritan, Roanoke, Terror, Maine, Texas.		Ajax, Camanche, Catskill, Canonicus, Jason, Lehigh, Mahopac, Manhattan, Montauk, Nahant, Nantucket, Passaic, Wyandotte.		
Outfit.	Stores, 1 year.	Outfit.	Stores, 1 year.	Outfit.	Stores, 1 year.	Outfit.	Stores, 1 year.	Outfit.	Stores, 1 year.	Outfit.	Stores, 1 year.	
......	6	......	3	......	6	......	3	......	3	......	3	All tools to be handled and fitted for immediate use.
2	......	......	......	2	......	2	......	2	......	2	......	
......	2	......	2	......	2	......	2	......	2	......	2	
50	......	25	......	......	......	60	......	150	......	100	......	Of 40 pounds capacity.
......	2	......	1	......	2	......	2	......	2	......	2	For use in storerooms.
......	40	......	12	......	80	......	21	......	24	......	24	
......	12	......	6	......	15	......	12	......	18	......	15	Calcimining-brush pattern.
......	......	......	......	......	......	......	......	......	......	......	......	Sufficient for one-fourth the complement of officers and crew.
......	18	......	6	......	25	......	18	......	24	......	20	Fitted for candles only.
......	2	......	......	......	3	......	1	......	2	......	1	
......	......	......	......	......	......	......	......	......	......	......	......	As required.
......	......	......	......	......	......	......	......	......	......	......	......	Blacksmith's; as much as needed.
......	1	......	......	......	1	......	1	......	1	......	1	
3	2	2	......	3	2	2	1	......	......	......	......	
1	......	......	......	1	......	1	......	1	......	1	......	For fresh-water purposes.
3	......	2	......	4	......	3	......	4	......	3	......	To be placed in racks in different parts of ship below decks.
......	36	......	12	......	36	......	36	......	24	......	24	Chairs to be fitted to hook to bulkheads.
......	......	......	......	......	......	......	......	......	......	......	......	Three times the length of vessels between perpendiculars for three-decked vessels, twice for two decks, and one and one-half for single decks. From two to four sections of old hose will be put on board for washing decks.
27	......	......	......	30	......	27	......	27	......	27	......	In sections of nine feet length, with a strainer for one section.
......	70	......	12	......	80	......	70	......	80	......	70	Rubber.
1	......	......	......	1	......	1	......	......	......	......	......	Canvas, for carrying bilge-water to the scuppers. When required.
3	1	1	1	3	1	1	1	2	1	2	1	
......	2	......	1	......	2	......	2	......	2	......	2	Male and female.
1	......	......	......	1	......	1	......	1	......	1	......	Twelve copper expanding-rings furnished to each expander.
4	4	2	2	5	5	4	4	5	5	0	4	Composition.
......	......	......	......	......	......	......	......	......	......	......	......	The number allowed to be one-fifth the ship's company.
......	......	......	......	......	......	......	......	......	......	......	......	The number allowed to be one-fifth the ship's company.
......	1	......	½	......	2	......	1	......	2	......	1	
......	6	......	2	......	6	......	0	......	8	......	6	
......	10	......	......	......	......	......	......	......	40	......	25	
......	1	......	1	......	2	......	1	......	1	......	1	
......	12	......	......	......	15	......	......	......	......	......	......	

CARPENTER'S DEPARTMENT—Continued.

MISCELLANEOUS.	FIRST CLASS. Chicago, Philadelphia, Newark, San Francisco, and Class.		SECOND CLASS. Baltimore, Charleston.		THIRD CLASS. Brooklyn, Hartford, Lancaster, Pensacola, Richmond.		FOURTH CLASS. Boston, Atlanta, No. 7, No. 8, and Class.		FIFTH CLASS. Galena, Juniata, Marion, Mohican, Ossipee, Quinnebaug, Swatara, Omaha.		SIXTH CLASS. Iroquois, Kearsarge, Adams, Alliance, Essex, Enterprise, Nipsic.		SEVENTH CLASS. Yorktown, Concord, Bennington, No. 9, No. 10, No. 11, and Class.	
	Outfit.	Stores, 1 year.	Outfit.	Stores, 1 year.	Outfit.	Stores, 1 year.	Outfit.	Stores, 1 year.	Outfit.	Stores, 1 year.	Outfit.	Stores, 1 year.	Outfit.	Stores, 1 year.
Shovels		6		6		6		4		4		4		4
Stencil letters and numbers ... sets		1		1		1		1		1		1		1
Scrapers		80		70		70		60		60		50		50
Swifter-ropes for capstans														
Slings (canvas breeches)	2		2		2		2		2		2		1	
Spades		3		3		3		3		3		3		3
Squilgees	50		45		45		40		40		40		40	
Squilgee-plates (rubber)		50		45		45		40		40		40		40
Stoves (for hard coal), with platforms														
Trucks (iron)	2		2		2		2		2		2		2	
Turnbuckles (brass)		4		4		4		4		4		4		4
Wood, fire, clean														

CARPENTER'S DEPARTMENT—Continued.

		Eighth Class.		Ninth Class.		Sailing Vessels.		Paddle-wheel Steamers.		Ironclads. First Class.		Ironclads. Second Class.		Remarks.
		Alert, Ranger, Yantic, Petrel, and Chase.		Fortune, Leyden, Mayflower, Nina, Palos, Pinta, Speedwell, Standish, Triana, Intrepid, Alarm, Despatch, Vesuvius.		Constellation, Portsmouth, Jamestown.		Monocacy, Talapoosa, Michigan.		Amphitrite, Dictator, Miantonomoh, Monadnock, Puritan, Roanoke, Terror, Maine, Texas.		Ajax, Camanche, Catskill, Canonicus, Jason, Lehigh, Mahopac, Manhattan, Montauk, Nahant, Nantucket, Passaic, Wyandotte.		
		Outfit.	Stores, 1 year.	Outfit.	Stores, 1 year.	Outfit.	Stores, 1 year.	Outfit.	Stores, 1 year.	Outfit.	Stores, 1 year.	Outfit.	Stores, 1 year.	
			3		2		4		4		3		3	
			1		1		1		1		1		1	
			40		12		50		40		18		18	
														One for each capstan.
		1				2		1						
			2		1		3		2		2		2	One to be long-handled.
		36		12		40		24		36		36		Fitted with rubber plates and handles.
			36		12		40		24		36		36	
														As required when not heated by steam.
		2						2		2		2		For wheeling coal to scuttles.
			4				4		2					
														As much as can be stored.

CARPENTER'S DEPARTMENT—Continued.

Cooking-stoves.	Pots and covers.	Iron tea-kettles, enameled.	Dish-kettles and covers.	Spiders.	Griddles.	Gridirons.	Roasting-spits for oven.	Dippers.	Round pans.	Square pans.	Dripping-pans.	Pokers.	Lifters.
No.	No.	No.	No.	No.	No.	No.	No.	No.	No.	No.	No.	No.	No.
1	1	1	1	1	1	1	1	1	1	1	1	1	1

ADDITIONAL COOKING UTENSILS

Cook's knives.	Chopping-knives.	Sieves.	Chopping-dishes.	Soapstone griddles.	Colanders.	Roasting-pans.	Baking-pans.	Iron spoons.	Iron pots.	Tormentors, small.	Tea-kettles, copper.	Kneading-troughs.	Rolling-pins.
No.	No.	No.	No.	No.	No.	No.	No.	No.	No.	No.	No.	No.	No.
2	1	1	1	1	1	2	2	2	1	1	1	1	1

COOKING UTENSILS FOR COMMANDERS OF

Cook's knives.	Chopping-knives.	Sieves.	Chopping-dishes.	Iron griddles.	Soapstone griddles.	Colanders.	Roasting-pans.	Baking-pans.	Iron spoons.	Iron pots.	Tormentors, small.	Tea-kettles, copper.	Tea-kettles, iron, enameled.	Kneading-troughs.	Rolling-pins.	Pastry-boards.
No.	No.	No.	No.	No.	No.	No.	No.	No.	No.	No.	No.	No.	No.	No.	No.	No.
2	1	1	1	1	1	1	2	2	2	1	1	1	1	1	1	1

CARPENTERS' DEPARTMENT—Continued.

Shakers.	Scrapers.	Handle ash-pans.	Ash-pans.	Wood grates.	Spare coal grates and lining.	Flat-iron heaters.	Hot-water tanks.	Warming-closets.	Remarks.
No.	No.	No.	No.	No.	No.	No.	No.	No.	
1	1	1	1	1	1	1	1	1	

FURNISHED BY EQUIPMENT BUREAU.

Pastry-boards.	Pie-plates.	Frying-pans.	Fish-kettles.	Coffee-mills.	Skimmers.	Cake-turners.	Wood pestles.	Waffle-irons.	Wire broilers.	Baking-cups.	Coffee-boilers, tin.	Wash-pans.	Knife-trays.	Cleavers, small.	Knife-boards.	Sauce or stew pans, enameled.	Dredge-boxes, tin.	Remarks.
No.	No.	No.	No.	No.	No.	No.	No.	No.	No.	No.	No.	No.	No.	No.	No.	No.	No.	
1	6	2	1	1	1	1	1	1	2	12	1	1	1	1	1	4	1	

VESSELS NOT SUPPLIED WITH COOKING-STOVES.

Pie-plates.	Frying-pans.	Fish-kettles.	Coffee-mills.	Skimmers.	Cake-turners.	Wood pestles.	Waffle-irons.	Wire broilers.	Baking-cups.	Coffee-boilers, tin.	Wash-pans.	Knife-trays.	Cleavers, small.	Knife-boards.	Gridirons.	Sauce or stew pans, enameled.	Dredge-boxes, tin.	Remarks.
No.	No.	No.	No.	No.	No.	No.	No.	No.	No.	No.	No.	No.	No.	No.	No.	No.	No.	
6	2	1	1	1	1	1	1	1	6	1	1	1	1	1	1	4	1	

CARPENTER'S DEPARTMENT—Continued.

COOKING UTENSILS FOR CREW.

	Baking-pans, sheet-iron.	Copper coffee-boilers.*	Copper tea-kettles, large.	Skillets.	Coal-hods.	Sauce or stew-pans.	Sconse-kettles (enameled).	Frying-pans.	Iron spoons, large and small.	Cleavers, small.
	No.	No.	No.	No.	No.	No.	No.	No.	No.	No.
1st and 2d classes, and 1st class ironclads	10	2	1	2	3	10	30	10	6	1
3d and 4th classes	8	2	1	2	3	7	24	7	6	1
5th and 6th classes, and 2d class ironclads	8	2	1	2	3	7	18	7	6	1
7th and 8th classes	7	2	1	2	3	5	14	5	6	1

WARD-ROOM

GALLEY COOKING UTENSILS.

	Cook's knives.	Chopping-knives.	Sieves.	Chopping-dishes.	Soapstone griddles.	Iron griddles.	Colanders.	Roasting-pans.	Baking-pans.	Iron spoons.	Iron pots.	Tea-kettles, copper.	Kneading-troughs.	Rolling-pins.	Pastry-boards.	Pie-plates.
	No.	No.	No.	No.	No.	No.	No.	No.	No.	No.	No.	No.	No.	No.	No.	No.
1st and 2d classes, and 1st class ironclads	1	1	1	1	1	1	1	3	3	1	1	1	1	1	1	6
3d and 4th classes	1	1	1	1	1	1	1	3	3	1	1	1	1	1	1	6
5th and 6th classes, and 2d class ironclads	1	1	1	1	1	1	1	3	3	1	1	1	1	1	1	6
7th and 8th classes	1	1	1	1	1	1	1	3	3	1	1	1	1	1	1	6

STEERAGE AND

GALLEY COOKING UTENSILS.

Cook's knives.	Chopping-knives.	Sieves.	Chopping-dishes.	Soapstone griddles.*	Iron griddles.*	Colanders.	Roasting-pans.*	Baking-pans.*	Iron spoons.	Iron pots.*	Tea-kettles, copper.	Kneading-troughs.	Rolling-pins.	Pastry-boards.	Pie-plates.	Frying-pans.	Fish-kettles.	Coffee-mills.	Skimmers.	Cake-turners.	Wood-pestles.
No.	No.	No.	No.	No.	No.	No.	No.	No.	No.	No.	No.	No.	No.	No.	No.	No.	No.	No.	No.	No.	No.
2	2	2	2	*1	*1	2	*2	*2	2	*1	2	2	2	2	8	2	1	2	2	2	2

NOTE.—A special allowance will be authorized where galleys or ranges are provided.

CARPENTER'S DEPARTMENT—Continued.

Cooking utensils for crew.			Extra articles.			Remarks.
Knives and forks, ship's cook.	Candle-stands, tin.	Safety-matches, in tin boxes, gross.	Axes, wood.	Grate-bars, extra.	Soapstone linings, extra.	
No.	No.	No.	No.	Sets.	Sets.	
4	2	1	2	2	2	* Necessary officers' messes may make use of these boilers.
4	2	1	2	2	2	
4	2	1	2	2	2	
4	2	1	2	2	2	

OFFICERS.

GALLEY COOKING UTENSILS.

Frying-pans.	Fish-kettles.	Coffee-mills.	Skimmers.	Cake-turners.	Wood-pestles.	Waffle-irons.	Wire broilers.	Baking-cups.	Coffee-boilers, tin.	Wash-pans.	Knife-trays.	Cleavers.	Knife-boards.	Gridirons.	Sauce or stew-pans, enameled.	Tea-kettles, iron, enameled.	Dredge-boxes, tin.	Remarks.
No.	No.	No.	No.	No.	No.	No.	No.	No.	No.	No.	No.	No.	No.	No.	No.	No.	No.	
2	1	1	1	1	1	1	2	12	1	1	1	1	1	1	10	1	1	
2	1	1	1	1	1	1	2	12	1	1	1	1	1	1	10	1	1	
2	1	1	1	1	1	1	2	12	1	1	1	1	1	1	8	1	1	
2	1	1	1	1	1	1	2	12	1	1	1	1	1	1	8	1	1	

WARRANT OFFICERS.

GALLEY COOKING UTENSILS.

Waffle-irons.*	Wire broilers.*	Baking-cups.	Coffee-boilers, tin.	Wash-pans.	Knife-trays.	Cleavers.*	Knife-boards.	Gridirons.	Sauce or stew pans, enameled.	Tea-kettles, iron, enameled.*	Dredge boxes, tin.	Remarks.
No.	No.	No.	No.	No.	No.	No.	No.	No.	No.	No.	No.	
* 1	* 1	12	2	2	2	* 1	1	2	6	* 1	2	To be divided between the two messes. Those marked with a star are for joint use.

SAILMAKER'S DEPARTMENT.

Sails.	First Class. Chicago, Philadelphia, Newark, San Francisco, and Class.						Second Class. Baltimore and Charleston.						Third Class. Brooklyn, Hartford, Lancaster, Pensacola, Richmond.						Fourth Class. Boston, Atlanta, No. 7, No. 8, and Class.						Fifth Class. Galena, Marion, Mohican, Ossipee, Swatara, Omaha.						Sixth Class. Iroquois, Kearsarge, Adams, Alliance, Essex, Enterprise, Nipsic.						Seventh Class. Yorktown, Concord, Bennington, No. 9, No. 10, No. 11, and Class.					
	No. of sails.	No. of canvas.	Size of rope. Head.	Foot.	Leech.	Hoist.	No. of sails.	No. of canvas.	Size of rope. Head.	Foot.	Leech.	Hoist.	No. of sails.	No. of canvas.	Size of rope. Head.	Foot.	Leech.	Hoist.	No. of sails.	No. of canvas.	Size of rope. Head.	Foot.	Leech.	Hoist.	No. of sails.	No. of canvas.	Size of rope. Head.	Foot.	Leech.	Hoist.	No. of sails.	No. of canvas.	Size of rope. Head.	Foot.	Leech.	Hoist.	No. of sails.	No. of canvas.	Size of rope. Head.	Foot.	Leech.	Hoist.
Fore-sails	2	2	2¼	5¾	5¾								2	2	2¼	5½	5½		2	2	2¼	5½	5½		2	2	2¼	5¾	5¾		2	2	2¼	5	5							
Fore-topsails	2	2	2¼	5¾	4½								2	2	2¼	5½	4¾		2	2	2¼	5½	4½		2	2	2¼	5¼	4¾		2	2	2¼	5	4							
Fore-topgallant sails	2	4	2	3¼	2¾								2	4	2	3¼	2¾		2	4	2	3½	2¾		2	5	2	3¼	2¾		2	5	2	3	2¾							
Fore-royals													2	8	1¾	2¼	2¼								2	8	1¼	2½	2¼		2	8	1¼	2	2							
Main-sails	2	2	2¼	5½	5¾								2	2	2¼	5¾	5¼		2	2	2¼	5¼	5¼		2	2	2¼	5½	5½		2	2	2¼	5	5							
Main-topsails	2	2	2¼	5¾	4¾								2	2	2¼	5½	4½		2	2	2¼	5½	4½		2	2	2¼	5½	4½		2	2	2¼	5	4½							
Main-topgallant sails	2	4	2	3½	2¾								2	4	2	3½	2¾		2	4	2	3¼	2¾		2	5	1¾	3½	2¾		2	5	1¾	3	2½							
Main-royals													2	6	1¾	2¼	2¼								2	8	1½	2½	2¼		2	8	1½	2¼	2¼							
Mizzen-topsails													2	3	2¼	4¼	3								2	4	2¼	4	3		2	4	2¼	3¾	3							
Mizzen-topgallant sails													2	6	1¾	3	2½								2	7	1½	3	2½		2	7	1½	2¾	2½							
Mizzen-royals													2	9	1½	2¼	2¼								2	9	1¼	2	2		2	9	1¼	1¾	1¾							
Flying-jibs						2¾							2	5	--	2¾	2¾	2¾							2	6	--	2½	2½	2½	2	6	--	2¼	2¼	2¼						
Jibs	2	2	--	3½	3½	3½							2	2	--	3¼	3¼	3¼	2	2	--	3¼	3¼	3¼	2	3	--	3	3	3	2	3	--	2¾	2¾	2¾	2	3	--	2¾	2¾	2¾
Fore try-sails	1	1	2¼	3	3½	3							1	1	2¼	3	3½	3	1	1	2¼	3	3½	3	1	2	2¼	3	3¼	3	1	2	2¼	2¾	3	2¾	1	2	2¼	2¾	3	2¾
Main try-sails	2	1	2¼	3	3¾	3							2	1	2¼	3	3½	3	2	1	2¼	3	3½	3	2	2	2¼	3	3¼	3	2	2	2¼	2¾	3	2¾	2	2	2¼	2¾	3	2¾
Storm-mizzens	1	1	--	3½	3¼	3¼							1	1	--	3½	3¼	3¼							1	1	--	3	3	3	1	1	--	3	3	3	1	1	--	2¾	2¾	2¾
Spankers	2	2	2¼	3	3¾	3							2	2	2¼	3	3½	3							2	3	2¼	3	3¼	3	2	3	2¼	2¾	3	2¾	2	3	2¼	2¾	3	2¾
Fore-storm stay-sails	1	1	--	3¼	3¼	3¼	1	1	--	3¼	3¾	3¼	1	1	--	3¼	3¼	3¼	1	1	--	3½	3¼	3¼	1	1	--	3	3	3	1	1	--	3	3	3	1	1	--	2¾	2¾	2¾
Fore-topmast stay-sails	2	2	--	3½	3¼	3½							2	2	--	3½	3½	3¼	2	2	--	3¼	3½	3¼	2	2	--	3	3	3	2	2	--	3	3	3	2	2	--	2¾	2¾	2¾
Mizzen-storm stay-sails	1	1	--	3½	3¼	3½							1	1	--	3½	3½	3¼							1	1	--	3	3	3	1	1	--	3	3	3	1	1	--	2¾	2¾	2¾
Main-topmast stay-sails	1	7	--	2½	2½	2½							1	7	--	2½	2½	2½							1	8	--	2¼	2¼	2¼	1	8	--	2¼	2¼	2¼						
Mizzen-topmast stay-sails	1	7	--	2¼	2½	2½							1	7	--	2¼	2¼	2¼	1	7	--	2¼	2¼	2¼	1	8	--	2¼	2¼	2¼	1	8	--	2	2	2	1	8	--	2	2	2
Main-storm stay-sails	1	1	--	3¼	3¼	3¼	1	1	--	3¼	3¼	3¼	1	1	--	3¼	3¼	3¼	1	1	--	3¼	3¼	3¼	1	1	--	3	3	3	1	1	--	2¾	2¾	2¾	1	1	--	2¾	2¾	2¾
Gaff topsails																																					2	6	--	2½	2½	2½

NOTE.—The first four classes, including first-class sailing-vessels, will have

SAILMAKER'S DEPARTMENT—Continued.

	Eighth Class.						Ninth Class.						Sailing-vessels.												Paddle-wheel Steamers.						Remarks.
	Alert, Ranger, Yantic, Petrel, and Class.						Fortune, Leyden, Mayflower, Palos, Pinta, Speedwell, Standish, Despatch, Vesuvius.						Constellation.						Saratoga, Jamestown, Portsmouth.						Monocacy, Talapoosa, Michigan.						
	No. of sails.	No. of canvas.	Size of rope. Head.	Foot.	Leech.	Hoist.	No. of sails.	No. of canvas.	Size of rope. Head.	Foot.	Leech.	Hoist.	No. of sails.	No. of canvas.	Size of rope. Head.	Foot.	Leech.	Hoist.	No. of sails.	No. of canvas.	Size of rope. Head.	Foot.	Leech.	Hoist.	No. of sails.	No. of canvas.	Size of rope. Head.	Foot.	Leech.	Hoist.	
	2	2	2½	4½	4½	--	--	--	--	--	--	--	2	2	2½	5½	5½	--	2	2	2½	5	5	--	--	--	--	--	--	--	Fore-and-aft sails, as well as courses, topsails, and topgallant sails, are to be fitted with galvanized-iron clews, and shall have lip-thimbles at the eye-splices. Foot-ropes, in the wake of chafes, shall be covered with leather.
	2	2	2½	4½	3½	--	--	--	--	--	--	--	2	2	2½	5½	4½	--	2	2	2½	5	4	--	--	--	--	--	--	--	
	2	7	1¾	2¾	2½	--	--	--	--	--	--	--	2	4	2	3½	2¾	--	2	5	2	3	2½	--	--	--	--	--	--	--	
	2	9	1½	1¾	1¾	--	--	--	--	--	--	--	2	8	1¾	2½	2½	--	2	8	1½	2	2	--	--	--	--	--	--	--	
	2	3	2½	4½	4½	--	--	--	--	--	--	--	2	2	2½	5½	5½	--	2	2	2½	5	5	--	--	--	--	--	--	--	First and second reefs of topsails shall be French reefs with grab-lines; other reefs to be fitted with manilla points.
	2	2	2½	4½	3½	--	--	--	--	--	--	--	2	2	2½	5½	4½	--	2	2	2½	5	4	--	--	--	--	--	--	--	
	2	7	1¾	2¾	2½	--	--	--	--	--	--	--	2	4	2	3½	2¾	--	2	5	1¾	3	2½	--	--	--	--	--	--	--	Blocks in the head of fore-and-aft sails will be fitted with patent rollers.
	2	9	1½	1¾	1¾	--	--	--	--	--	--	--	2	8	1¾	2½	2½	--	2	8	1½	2	2	--	--	--	--	--	--	--	
	--	--	--	--	--	--	--	--	--	--	--	--	2	3	2½	4½	3	--	2	4	2½	3½	3	--	--	--	--	--	--	--	
	--	--	--	--	--	--	--	--	--	--	--	--	2	6	1¾	3	2½	--	2	7	1½	2¾	2½	--	--	--	--	--	--	--	
	--	--	--	--	--	--	--	--	--	--	--	--	2	9	1½	2½	2½	--	2	9	1½	1½	1¾	--	--	--	--	--	--	--	
	2	7	--	2	2	2	--	--	--	--	--	--	2	5	--	2¾	2¾	2½	2	6	--	2½	2½	2½	--	--	--	--	--	--	
	2	4	--	2½	2½	2½	--	--	--	--	--	--	2	2	--	3½	3½	3½	2	3	--	2¾	2¾	2¾	--	--	--	--	--	--	
	1	3	2	2½	2¾	2½	1	4	2	2½	2¾	2½	1	1	2½	3	3½	3	1	2	2½	2¾	3	2¾	1	3	2½	2¾	3½	2¾	
	2	3	2	2½	2¾	2½	1	4	2	2½	2¾	2½	2	1	2½	3	3½	3	2	2	2½	2¾	3	2¾	1	3	2½	2¾	3½	2¾	
	1	1	--	2¾	2¾	2¾	1	2	--	2¾	2¾	2¾	1	1	--	3½	3½	3½	1	1	--	3	3	3	1	1	--	3	3	3	
	2	4	2	2½	2¾	2½	--	--	--	--	--	--	2	2	2½	3	3½	3	2	3	2½	2¾	3	2½	--	--	--	--	--	--	
	1	1	--	2¾	2¾	2¾	1	2	--	2½	2½	2¾	1	1	--	3½	3½	3½	1	1	--	3	3	3	1	1	--	3	3	3	
	2	2	--	2¾	2¾	2¾	*1	6	--	2½	2½	2½	2	2	--	3½	3½	3½	2	2	--	3	3	3	*1	5	--	2½	2½	2½	* Fore stay-sail.
	1	1	--	2¾	2¾	2¾	--	--	--	--	--	--	1	1	--	3½	3½	3½	1	1	--	3	3	3	--	--	--	--	--	--	
	1	8	--	2½	2½	2½	--	--	--	--	--	--	1	7	--	2½	2½	2½	1	8	--	2½	2½	2½	--	--	--	--	--	--	When required.
	1	8	--	2	2	2	--	--	--	--	--	--	1	7	--	2½	2½	2½	1	6	--	2	2	2	--	--	--	--	--	--	
	1	1	--	2¾	2¾	2¾	--	--	--	--	--	--	1	1	--	3½	3½	3½	1	1	--	3	3	3	--	--	--	--	--	--	When required.
	2	6	--	2½	2½	2½	2	7	--	2½	2½	2½	--	--	--	--	--	--	--	--	--	--	--	--	2	7	--	2½	2½	2½	

one fore sail, one fore topsail, and one main-topsail of No. 1 canvas.

SAILMAKER'S DEPARTMENT—Continued.

Miscellaneous.	First Class.	Second Class.	Third Class.	Fourth Class.	Fifth Class.	Sixth Class.	Seventh Class.
	Chicago, Philadelphia, Newark, San Francisco, and Class.	Baltimore, Charleston.	Brooklyn, Hartford, Lancaster, Pensacola, Richmond.	Boston, Atlanta, No. 7, No. 8, and Class.	Galena, Juniata, Marion, Mohican, Ossipee, Quinnebaug, Swatara, Omaha.	Iroquois, Kearsarge, Adams, Alliance, Essex, Enterprise, Nipsic.	Yorktown, Concord, Bennington, No. 9, No. 10, No. 11, and Class.
	1 year.	1 year.	1 year.	1 year.	1 year.	1 year.	1 year.
Awnings, ships' .... set.	1	1	1	1	1	1	1
Beeswax for twine .... pounds.	20	20	20	20	20	15	15
Bags, clothes	....	....	....	....	....	....	....
Bags, hammock	....	....	....	....	....	....	....
Bags, pea-jacket	10	10	10	10	10	10	8
Bags, mess	....	....	....	....	....	....	....
Bags, coal	....	....	....	....	....	....	....
* Bags, coaling	8	8	8	8	8	8	8
Canvas, cotton, No. 1 .... bolts.	....	....	½	....	½	½	....
Canvas, cotton, No. 2 .... do.	½	....	....	½	....	....	½
Canvas, cotton, No. 4 .... do.	2	1	2	1	1	1	½
Canvas, cotton, No. 5 .... do.	1	1	1	1	1	½	1
Canvas, cotton, No. 6 .... do.	....	....	....	....	....	....	....
Canvas, cotton, No. 8 .... do.	½	½	½	½	½	½	½
Canvas, cotton, bag .... do.	1	1	1	1	½	½	½
Canvas, cotton, No. 10 .... do.	½	....	½	½	½	....	....
Canvas, flax, No. 1 .... do.	½	½	½	½	½	½	....
Canvas, flax, No. 2 .... do.	1	....	2	1	1	1	½
Canvas, flax, No. 3 .... do.	½	....	1	½	1	1	½
Canvas, flax, No. 4 .... do.	1	½	1	1	1	1	½
Canvas, flax, No. 5 .... do.	½	....	1	½	½	½	....
Canvas, flax, No. 6 .... do.	½	....	1	½	1	1	....
Canvas, flax, No. 7 .... do.	½	½	½	½	½	½	½
Canvas, flax, No. 8 .... do.	1	1	1	1	1	1	1
Canvas, old .... yards.	500	500	500	500	300	300	100
Clews, iron, galvanized	6	....	6	6	6	6	4
Cloths, bunt, topsails	....	....	....	....	....	....	....
Cloths, hammock, blacked .... set.	1	1	1	1	1	1	1
Covers, hammock-box .... do.	....	....	....	....	....	....	....

* To be of No. 1 flax canvas, doubled and roped.

SAILMAKER'S DEPARTMENT—Continued.

Eighth Class.	Ninth Class.	Sailing Vessels.	Paddle-wheel Steamers.	Ironclads. First Class.	Ironclads. Second Class.	Remarks.
Alert, Ranger, Yantic, Petrel, and Class.	Fortune, Leyden, Mayflower, Nina, Palos, Pinta, Speedwell, Standish, Triana, Intrepid, Alarm, Despatch, Vesuvius.	Constellation, Portsmouth, Jamestown.	Monocacy, Talapoosa, Michigan.	Amphitrite, Dictator, Miantonomoh, Monadnock, Puritan, Roanoke, Terror, Maine, Texas.	Ajax, Camanche, Catskill, Canonicus, Jason, Lehigh, Mahopac, Manhattan, Montauk, Nahant, Nantucket, Passaic, Wyandotte.	
1 year.	1 year.	1 year.	1 year.	1 year.	1 year.	
1	1	1	1	1	1	First six classes of No. 4 cotton canvas; other classes, including monitors and 2d-class paddle-wheel steamers, of No. 5.
15	2	15	2	5	5	
						One black and one white bag allowed for each man and boy of the vessel's complement, except where lockers are provided, when two white bags will be allowed.
						One for each gun's crew; of No. 6 flax canvas.
8	1	10	2	5	4	Of No. 5 flax canvas.
						One for each berth-deck mess, of No. 7 flax canvas.
						Coal-bags of gunny cloth; not to be put on board or purchased, unless necessary for carrying extra coal.
4			2			Eight allowed for masted iron-clads.
		½				
½		½	½	½	½	A bolt of canvas in this table is to be of 80 yards; but where the bolt consists of 40 yards, the allowance will be doubled.
1	½	4		½	½	
½		½				
½		½	½	½	½	A bolt of bag-canvas to contain 100 running yards.
			½			
½		1				
1		2				
1		3				
½		1½	1			
	½	1				
1		1				
½		1	½			
1		1	¼	1	1	
200	50	300	100	100	75	
4		6	2			For topsails and courses.
						Of No. 3 or No. 4 flax canvas, one set as required.
1		1	1			No. 4 cotton canvas.
	1			1	1	No. 4 cotton canvas.

SAILMAKER'S DEPARTMENT—Continued.

MISCELLANEOUS.	FIRST CLASS.	SECOND CLASS.	THIRD CLASS.	FOURTH CLASS.	FIFTH CLASS.	SIXTH CLASS.	SEVENTH CLASS.
	Chicago, Philadelphia, Newark, San Francisco, and Class.	Baltimore, Charleston.	Brooklyn, Hartford, Lancaster, Pensacola, Richmond.	Boston, Atlanta, No. 7, No. 8, and Class.	Galena, Juniata, Marion, Mohican, Ossipee, Quinnebaug, Swatara, Omaha.	Iroquois, Kearsarge, Adams, Alliance, Essex, Enterprise, Nipsic.	Yorktown, Concord, Bennington, No. 9, No. 10, No. 11, and Class.
	1 year.	1 year.	1 year.	1 year.	1 year.	1 year.	1 year.
Commanders, iron	3	3	3	3	3	3	2
Cots, cabin	4	4	4	2	2	2	2
Cots, ward-room	8	8	8	6	6	4	4
Cots, hospital	12	12	10	8	8	6	6
Covers, head	----	----	----	----	----	----	----
Covers, boom	----	----	1	1	1	1	----
Covers, binnacle	3	3	3	3	3	3	3
Covers, skylight	----	----	----	----	----	----	----
Covers, capstan	----	----	----	----	----	----	----
Covers, sail, fore-and-aft	----	----	----	----	----	----	----
Covers, mainmast	1	1	1	1	1	1	1
Cover, mainsail	1	1	1	1	1	1	1
Cover, main-topsail	1	1	1	1	1	1	1
Covers, top and chain-chests	----	----	----	----	----	----	----
Covers, wheel	1	1	1	1	1	1	1
Covers, reel ....one set.	----	----	----	----	----	----	----
Covers, windsail	----	----	----	----	----	----	----
Curtains, awning	----	----	----	----	----	----	----
Dividers, drafting	1	1	1	1	1	1	1
Duck, ravens, cotton ....bolts.	1	½	1	1	1	1	1
Duck, ravens, flax ....do.	1	½	1	1	1	1	1
Fids, setting	2	2	2	2	2	1	½
Fids, splicing	6	6	10	10	8	8	6
Hammock numbers	----	----	----	----	----	----	----
Hammocks ....sets.	1	1	1	1	1	1	1
Hammock canvas ....bolts.	1	1	1	1	1	1	½
Hoods for hammock nettings ....set.	1	1	1	1	1	1	1
Hoods for hatches	----	----	----	----	----	----	----
Hooks, sail	6	8	8	8	6	6	5
Knives, sail	8	8	8	8	6	6	5
Leather, bellows, sides	1	1	3	3	2	2	1
Line, measuring	2	1	1	1	1	1	1
Needles, seaming	150	150	150	125	125	125	----

SAILMAKER'S DEPARTMENT—Continued.

Eighth Class.	Ninth Class.	Sailing Vessels.	Paddle-wheel Steamers.	Ironclads. First Class.	Ironclads. Second Class.	Remarks.
Alert, Ranger, Yantic, Petrel, and Class.	Fortune, Leyden, Mayflower, Nina, Palos, Pinta, Speedwell, Standish, Triana, Intrepid, Alarm, Despatch, Vesuvius.	Constellation, Portsmouth, Jamestown.	Monocacy, Talapoosa, Michigan.	Amphitrite, Dictator, Miantonomoh, Monadnock, Puritan, Roanoke, Terror, Maine, Texas.	Ajax, Camanche, Catskill, Canonicus, Jason, Lehigh, Mahopac, Manhattan, Montauk, Nahant, Nantucket, Passaic, Wyandotte.	
1 year.	1 year.	1 year.	1 year.	1 year.	1 year.	
2	—	3	1	1	1	Assorted sizes.
2	—	2	2	1	1	
3	1	4	2	4	3	
4	1	6	2	6	4	
—	—	—	—	—	—	No. 4 cotton canvas, painted; allowed only to vessels where the head is exposed.
—	—	1	—	—	—	No. 4 cotton canvas, unpainted.
3	—	3	1	1	1	No. 6 cotton canvas, oiled.
—	—		—	—	—	As required; No. 6 cotton canvas, oiled.
—	—	—	—	—	—	No. 6 cotton canvas, oiled. Allowed for exposed wooden capstans.
—	—	—	—	—	—	One for each sail; No. 6 cotton canvas.
1	—	—	—	—	—	No. 4 flax canvas, unpainted.
1	—	—	—	—	—	No. 4 flax canvas, unpainted.
1	—	—	—	—	—	No. 4 flax canvas, unpainted.
—	—	—	—	—	—	One for each chest; No. 5 cotton canvas, painted.
1	—	1	—	1	1	No. 6 cotton canvas, oiled.
—	—	—	—	—	—	No. 6 cotton canvas, unpainted.
—	—	—	—	—	—	One for each windsail; No. 6 cotton canvas.
—	—	—	—	—	—	A set for one side only.
1	—	1	1	1	1	
1	1	2	1	1	1	
1	—	1	1	1	1	
1	—	2	1	1	1	
6	2	8	2	6	6	
—	—	—	—	—	—	No. 10 cotton canvas; spare set for crew.
1	1	1	1	1	1	To be $3\frac{1}{2}$ by 6 feet; of hammock canvas.
$\frac{1}{2}$	—	1	—	1	$\frac{1}{3}$	
1	—	1	1	—	—	No. 4 cotton canvas, painted black.
—	—	—	—	—	—	Of No. 4 cotton canvas, oiled; for all hatches having frames or canopies.
5	2	6	2	2	2	
5	2	6	2	2	2	
1	—	2	—	—	—	
1	1	1	1	1	1	Wire-woven, 100 feet long.
100	10	125	10	20	10	Assorted—Nos. 14, 15, 16, and 17.

SAILMAKER'S DEPARTMENT—Continued.

Miscellaneous.	First Class.	Second Class.	Third Class.	Fourth Class.	Fifth Class.	Sixth Class.	Seventh Class.
	Chicago, Philadelphia, Newark, San Francisco, and Class.	Baltimore, Charleston.	Brooklyn, Hartford, Lancaster, Pensacola, Richmond.	Boston, Atlanta, No. 7, No. 8, and Class.	Galena, Juniata, Marion, Mohican, Ossipee, Quinnebaug, Swatara, Omaha.	Iroquois, Kearsarge, Adams, Alliance, Essex, Enterprise, Nipsic.	Yorktown, Concord, Bennington, No. 9, No. 10, No. 11, and Class.
	1 year.	1 year.	1 year.	1 year.	1 year.	1 year.	1 year.
Needles, 4-thread	15	----------	25	20	20	20	15
Needles, 6-thread	15	----------	20	15	15	15	8
Needles, 8-thread	5	----------	15	10	10	10	5
Palms, roping, mounted	10	----------	10	8	8	8	7
Palms, seaming, mounted	10	10	20	16	16	16	14
Prickers, sail	8	8	8	8	6	6	5
Rope, bolt, 1-inch ... fathoms	40	20	46	40	40	40	30
Rope, bolt, 1½-inch ... do	30	----------	50	46	46	40	30
Rope, bolt, 2-inch ... do	30	----------	38	36	30	35	25
Rope, bolt, 2¼-inch ... do	18	----------	19	18	18	17	17
Rope, bolt, 2½-inch ... do	40	20	75	45	70	70	65
Rope, bolt, 2¾-inch ... do	40	25	35	35	30	30	28
Rope, bolt, 3-inch ... do	10	----------	12	10	10	10	10
Rope, bolt, 3¼-inch ... do	18	----------	19	18	18	17	17
Rope, bolt, 4-inch ... do	----------	----------	----------	----------	----------	15	----------
Rope, bolt, 4¼-inch ... do	24	----------	24	24	24	----------	----------
Rope, bolt, 4½-inch ... do	16	----------	16	16	16	----------	16
Rope, bolt, 4¾-inch ... do	----------	----------	----------	----------	----------	----------	----------
Rope, bolt, 5-inch ... do	----------	----------	----------	----------	----------	20	----------
Rope, bolt, 5¼-inch ... do	20	----------	20	20	18	----------	----------
Rope, bolt, 5½-inch ... do	20	----------	20	20	----------	----------	----------
Rope, bolt, 5¾-inch ... do	----------	----------	----------	----------	----------	----------	----------
Rope, manila, 1½-inch ... do	25	----------	50	25	45	45	46
Rope, manila, 1¾-inch ... do	45	----------	50	45	45	45	20
Rope, manila, 2-inch ... do	40	40	75	75	75	----------	----------
Rules, two-foot ... each	1	1	1	1	1	1	1
Sails, smoke	1	1	1	1	1	1	1
Sails, wind (complete)	----------	----------	----------	----------	----------	----------	----------
Scales, Gunter	1	1	1	1	1	1	1
Shears, 10-inch	1	1	1	1	1	1	1
Squares, brass	1	1	1	1	1	1	1
Screens, gang-way ladder	----------	----------	----------	----------	----------	----------	----------
Screens, ladder	----------	----------	----------	----------	----------	----------	----------
Screens, top-gallant-forecastle	----------	----------	----------	----------	----------	----------	----------

SAILMAKER'S DEPARTMENT—Continued.

EIGHTH CLASS.	NINTH CLASS.	SAILING VESSELS.	PADDLE-WHEEL STEAMER.	IRONCLADS. FIRST CLASS.	IRONCLADS. SECOND CLASS.	REMARKS.
Alert, Ranger, Yantic, Petrel, and Class.	Fortune, Leyden, Mayflower, Nina, Palos, Pinta, Speedwell, Standish, Triana, Intrepid, Alarm, Despatch, Vesuvius.	Constellation, Portsmouth, Jamestown.	Monocacy, Talapoosa, Michigan.	Amphitrite, Dictator, Miantonomoh, Monadnock, Puritan, Roanoke, Terror, Maine, Texas.	Ajax, Camanche, Catskill, Canonicus, Jason, Lehigh, Mahopac, Manhattan, Montauk, Nahant, Nantucket, Passaic, Wyandotte.	
1 year.	1 year.	1 year.	1 year.	1 year.	1 year.	
15	5	15	6	6	6	
8	2	8	3	2	2	
8	2	10	2	2	2	
7	2	8	2	2	2	Best steel plate.
14	4	16	4	4	4	Best steel plate.
5	2	7	2	2	2	
35	10	40	20	30	20	
35	10	46	35	30	20	
50	10	30	25	30	25	
15	10	18	13	15	13	
65	—	75	55	40	40	
28	—	35	—	—	—	
8	—	10	—	—	—	
15	—	18	—	—	—	
—	—	15	—	—	—	
24	—	—	—	—	—	
—	—	—	—	—	—	
—	—	—	—	—	—	
—	—	20	—	—	—	
—	—	20	—	—	—	
—	—	—	—	—	—	
—	—	—	—	—	—	
40	10	45	10	—	—	For reef-points.
35	—	45	—	—	—	For reef-points.
—	—	—	—	—	—	For reef points.
1	1	1	1	1	1	
—	1	1	1	—	—	No. 4 flax canvas, unpainted.
—	—	—	—	—	—	One for each hatch, cabin, and ward-room sky-light.
1	1	1	1	1	1	
1	1	1	1	1	1	
1	1	1	1	1	1	Marked inches and eighths.
—	—	—	—	—	—	One for each ladder on starboard side, of No. 8 cotton canvas, unpainted.
—	—	—	—	—	—	For cabin and ward-room hatches only; No. 8 cotton canvas, unpainted.
—	—	—	—	—	—	No. 7 flax canvas, unpainted, when required.

SAILMAKER'S DEPARTMENT—Continued.

MISCELLANEOUS.	FIRST CLASS.	SECOND CLASS.	THIRD CLASS.	FOURTH CLASS.	FIFTH CLASS.	SIXTH CLASS.	SEVENTH CLASS.
	Chicago, Philadelphia, Newark, San Francisco, and Class.	Baltimore, Charleston.	Brooklyn, Hartford, Lancaster, Pensacola, Richmond.	Boston, Atlanta, No. 7, No. 8, and Class.	Galena, Juniata, Marion, Mohican, Ossipee, Quinnebaug, Swatara, Omaha.	Iroquois, Kearsarge, Adams, Alliance, Essex, Enterprise, Nipsic.	Yorktown, Concord, Bennington, No. 9, No. 10, No. 11, and Class.
	1 year.	1 year.	1 year.	1 year.	1 year.	1 year.	1 year.
Screens, galley							
Screens, head							
Slings, channel	2	2	2	2	2	2	2
Tallow ... pounds	10	10	10	8	8	8	6
Tarpaulins, hatch							
Tarpaulins							
Twine, cotton ... pounds	40	40	40	40	40	30	30
Twine, flax ... do	18	18	18	16	16	14	14
Yard-sticks	2	2	2	2	2	2	2

SAILMAKER'S DEPARTMENT—Continued.

Eighth Class.	Ninth Class.	Sailing Vessels.	Paddle-wheel Steamers.	Ironclads. First Class.	Ironclads. Second Class.	Remarks.
Alert, Ranger, Yantic, Petrel, and Clase.	Fortune, Leyden, Mayflower, Nina, Palos, Pinta, Speedwell, Standish, Triana, Intrepid, Alarm, Despatch, Vesuvius.	Constellation, Portsmouth, Jamestown.	Monocacy, Tallapoosa, Michigan.	Amphitrite, Dictator, Miantonomoh, Monadnock, Puritan, Roanoke, Terror, Maine, Texas.	Ajax, Camanche, Catskill, Canonicus, Jason, Lehigh, Mahopac, Manhattan, Montauk, Nahant, Nantucket, Passaic, Wyandotte.	
1 year.	1 year.	1 year.	1 year.	1 year.	1 year.	
----	----	----	----	----	----	When galley is under the break of top-gallant forecastle, No. 8 flax canvas, unpainted.
----	----	----	----	----	----	One set, No. 4 cotton canvas, when required.
2	----	2	2	2	2	No. 1 flax canvas, three thicknesses, unpainted.
6	3	8	3	3	3	
----	----	----	----	----	----	One for each spar and gun-deck hatch, fore and main holds, and, when needed, for other lower-deck hatches.
----	----	----	----	----	----	Two each for paymaster's yeoman and ship's cook.
30	4	30	6	10	8	Cotton twine, to be used for stitching and roping.
12	1[illegible]	14	2	6	4	Flax twine, for whipping and marling.
2	1	2	1	1	1	

TESTS FOR FLAX CANVAS.

Flax canvas to be 20 inches wide, and each bolt to contain 80 running yards. The blue thread in Nos. 1, 2, 3, and 4 to be 1⅝ inches from the selvage; in Nos. 5, 6, and 7, to be 1⅜ inches; in Nos. 8 and 9, 1 inch from selvage. The warp and filling to be spun exclusively of long, well-dressed, water-rolled flax, of the best quality, without any mixture of shorts or tow; the yarns evenly spun and of proper fineness; the warp to be rather more twisted than the filling. The warp and filling from Nos. 1 to 4, inclusive, to be double thread; Nos. 5 and 6, double warp and single filling; Nos. 7, 8, and 9, single warp and filling. No description of weaver's dressing, or any pressing or beating to be used in the manufacture. In testing, three strips crosswise and three strips lengthwise will be cut 1½ inches wide and 20 inches long, except in Nos. 8 and 9, which will be cut 2 inches wide and 20 inches long. The strips from 1 to 7, inclusive, must be raveled to 1 inch wide; 8 and 9, to 1½ inches wide, care being taken while raveling the strips for testing that the excess of thread in determining the width of the strip shall be given the strip being tested.

Canvas.	Weight per bolt.	Weight to be borne by strips.	
	Pounds avoirdupois.	Crosswise.	Lengthwise.
		Pounds.	*Pounds.*
Flax canvas, No. 1	84	470	316
Flax canvas, No. 2	76	420	280
Flax canvas, No. 3	70	370	250
Flax canvas, No. 4	64	340	230
Flax canvas, No. 5	58	320	216
Flax canvas, No. 6	52	300	200
Flax canvas, No. 7	46	280	193
Flax canvas, No. 8	40	300	200
Flax canvas, No. 9	34	280	193

TESTS FOR COTTON CANVAS.

Cotton canvas to be 22 inches wide, and to contain 80 running yards to the bolt. In Nos 1, 2, and 3 the blue thread must be 1½ inches from the selvage; in Nos. 4, 5, and 6, 1¼ inches; in Nos. 7 and 8, 1 inch; in Nos. 9 and 10, ¾ inch; in cotton ravens, ⅝ inch from the selvage. The filling should be stronger than the warp in all numbers. In testing, three strips crosswise and three strips lengthwise will be cut 1½ inches wide and 20 inches long, except in Nos. 8, 9, and 10, which will be cut 2 inches wide and 20 inches long. The strips from 1 to 7, inclusive, must be raveled to 1 inch wide; from 8 to 10, inclusive, to 1½ inches wide, care being taken while raveling the strips for testing that the excess of thread in determining the width of the strip shall be given the strip being tested. All ravens should have 35 running yards to the bolt, 28½ inches wide. The strips for testing to be cut the same width and length as Nos. 8 and 9 cotton canvas.

Canvas.	Weight per bolt.	Weight to be borne by strips.	
	Pounds avoirdupois.	Crosswise.	Lengthwise.
		Pounds.	*Pounds.*
Cotton canvas, No. 1	90	280	250
Cotton canvas, No. 2	85	260	230
Cotton canvas, No. 3	80	240	210
Cotton canvas, No. 4	75	230	200
Cotton canvas, No. 5	70	220	190
Cotton canvas, No. 6	65	210	180
Cotton canvas, No. 7	60	200	170
Cotton canvas, No. 8	55	220	190
Cotton canvas, No. 9	50	210	180
Cotton canvas, No. 10	45	200	170
Heavy cotton ravens	* 27	140	118
Light cotton ravens	† 22	90	81

* = 10-ounce duck. † = 12-ounce duck.

TESTS FOR HAMMOCK, BAG, AND COT DUCK.

The hammock and bag canvas to be 42 inches wide; the cot canvas to be 30 inches wide, and each bolt to contain 100 running yards. The blue thread to be 1¼ inches from the selvage in the hammock canvas, 1 inch in the bag canvas, and ⅝ inch from the selvage in the cot canvas. In testing, three strips crosswise and three strips lengthwise will be cut 1½ inches wide and 20 inches long in the hammock and bag, and 2 inches wide and 20 inches long in the cot canvas. The strips in the hammock and bag canvas to be raveled to 1 inch wide; the strips in the cot canvas to 1½ inches wide, care being taken while raveling the strips for testing that the excess of thread in determining the width of the strip shall be given to the strip being tested.

Canvas.	Weight per bolt.	Weight to be borne by strips.	
	Pounds.	Crosswise.	Lengthwise.
		Pounds.	*Pounds.*
Hammock duck = 1	215	280	250
Bag duck = 4	179	230	200
Cot duck = 8	100	220	190

Cabin cots to be cut 6 feet 2 inches long and 40 inches wide. All other cots to be cut 6 feet 2 inches long and 30 inches wide. Bottoms of all cots will be made of bag duck.

All canvas to be marked and distinguished as required by act of Congress approved July 17, 1862.

BOAT OUTFITS AND STORES.

Boatswain's, Sailmaker's, and Carpenter's departments.

Department.	Articles.	Steam-launches or steam-cutters.	Sailing-launches and 1st cutters.	All other cutters.	Gigs and whale-boats.	Remarks.
BOATSWAIN'S	Anchors .... each	1	1	1	1	See page 12.
	Anchor chains or ropes .... do	1	1	1	1	See pages 13 and 14.
	Hand-grapnels .... do	1	1	1	1	Fitted with 1 fathom of light chain and 5 fathoms of line.
	Hand-grapnel lines .... do	1	1	1	1	
	Painters .... do	1	1	1	1	
	Marline-spikes .... do	1	1	1	1	
	Spun-yarn .... balls	1	1	1	1	Two-yarn.
	Tallow .... pounds	1	1	1	1	
	Thrum-mats for oars .... sets	—	1	1	1	
	Trailing-lines .... do	—	1	1	1	9-thread hemp.
	Fishing-lines .... each	3	3	3	2	
	Fishing-hooks .... do	12	12	12	12	Assorted sizes.
	Grommets .... set	1	1	—	—	
	Lanyards for thole-pins .... do	1	1	—	—	6-thread hemp.
CARPENTER'S	Boat-stoves in packing-boxes .... each	1	1	—	—	1st cutters of three first classes only allowed stoves; boats without stoves allowed one stew-pan each.
	Boat-stove cooking-utensils .... set	1	1	—	—	
	Safety-matches .... boxes	1	1	1	1	
	Fenders, leather, with lanyards .... set	1	—	1	1	
	Fenders, rope, with lanyards .... do	—	1	—	—	
	Fenders, pudding	1	—	—	—	
	Fuel	—	—	—	—	As required.
SAILMAKER'S	Awnings .... each	—	1	1	1	Nos. 9 and 10 cotton canvas.
	Awning-bags .... do	—	1	1	1	Of No. 6 cotton canvas, painted lead-color.
	Arm-curtains .... set	—	—	—	—	One for each boat.
	Boat-covers .... each	—	—	1	1	Nos. 7 and 8 cotton, for boats at davits only.
	Cushions .... set	—	—	—	—	One set allowed each barge and gig, and two sets for running boats, of heavy cotton ravens, upper side of enameled cloth, stuffed with hair.
	Cushion-covers .... do	—	—	—	—	Of heavy sheeting. Two for each set of cushions.
	Cushion-bags .... each	1	1	1	1	Of No. 6 cotton canvas, painted lead-color.
	Canopies	1	—	—	—	Of No. 5 cotton canvas, unpainted. Weather-cloths of canvas allowed each steam-launch and cutter.
	Sails .... suit	1	1	1	1	Launches and 1st cutters of heavy cotton ravens; other boats, light cotton ravens.
	Sail-covers .... set	—	1	1	1	Nos. 7 and 8 cotton canvas.
	Tarpaulins	1	1	1	1	

STATIONERY.

Allowances for Equipment Officers.

Articles.	First Class.	Second Class.	Third Class.	Fourth Class.	Fifth Class.	Sixth Class.	Seventh Class.
	Chicago, Philadelphia, Newark, San Francisco, and Class.	Baltimore, Charleston.	Brooklyn, Hartford, Lancaster, Pensacola, Richmond.	Boston, Atlanta, No. 7, No. 8, and Class.	Galena, Juniata, Marion, Mohican, Ossipee, Quinnebaug, Swatara, Omaha.	Iroquois, Kearsarge, Adams, Alliance, Essex, Enterprise, Nipsic.	Yorktown, Concord, Bennington, No. 9, No. 10, No. 11, and Class.
	3 years.	3 years.	3 years.	3 years.	3 years.	3 years.	3 years.
Books, blank 3-quire	3	3	3	3	3	3	2
Books, watch and station 1-quire	3	3	3	3	3	3	2
Books, memorandum .... number	12	12	12	12	12	9	9
Blank surveys	75	75	75	75	75	75	75
Blank quarterly coal reports	36	36	36	36	36	36	36
Black ink .... pints	6	6	6	6	5	5	4
Envelopes, official .... packages	6	6	6	6	6	6	6
Envelopes, letter .... do	6	6	6	6	6	6	6
Eyes, metallic .... boxes	3	3	3	3	3	3	3
Gum-elastic loops .... dozen	6	6	6	6	6	6	6
India rubber .... pieces	6	6	6	6	6	6	6
Inkstands, heavy glass .... number	2	2	2	2	2	2	2
Memorandum-pads .... do	6	6	6	6	6	6	6
Mucilage .... half pints	3	3	3	3	3	3	3
Paper, drawing .... sheets	9	9	9	9	9	9	9
Paper, blotting .... do	24	24	24	24	24	24	24
Paper, foolscap .... reams	2	2	2	2	2	2	2
Paper, letter .... do	1	1	1	1	1	1	1
Paper, note .... do	½	½	½	½	½	½	½
Paper, regulation .... do	1	1	1	1	1	1	1
Pens, steel .... gross	2	2	2	2	2	2	2
Pen-holders .... dozen	2	2	2	2	2	2	2
Pencils, black lead .... do	3	3	3	3	3	3	3
Pencils, red and blue, assorted .... number	6	6	6	6	6	6	6
Red ink .... vials	2	2	2	2	2	2	2
Rulers, flat .... number	2	2	2	2	2	2	2
Tape .... pieces	6	6	6	6	6	6	6

STATIONERY.

Allowances for Equipment Officers.

Eighth Class.	Ninth Class.	Sailing Vessels.	Paddle-wheel Steamers.	Ironclads.		Remarks.
				First Class.	Second Class.	
Alert, Ranger, Yantic, Petrel, and Class.	Fortune, Leyden, Mayflower, Nina, Palos, Pinta, Speedwell, Standish, Triana, Intrepid, Alarm, Despatch, Vesuvius.	Constellation, Portsmouth, Jamestown.	Monocacy, Talapoosa, Michigan.	Amphitrite, Dictator, Miantonomoh, Monadnock, Puritan, Roanoke, Terror, Maine, Texas.	Ajax, Camanche, Catskill, Canonicus, Jason, Lehigh, Mahopac, Manhattan, Montauk, Nahant, Nantucket, Passaic, Wyandotte.	
3 years.	3 years.	3 years.	3 years.	3 years.	3 years.	
2	----	2	1	3	2	The allowances of this table are for three years; if a vessel is commissioned for a less time, the allowances will be reduced proportionately.
2	----	2	1	3	2	
8	4	9	6	12	9	
75	18	75	18	45	45	
36	30	----	36	36	36	
4	2	5	4	5	4	
6	2	6	6	6	0	
6	2	6	6	0	6	Two sizes.
6	1	3	3	3	3	
6	3	6	6	6	6	
6	3	6	6	6	6	
2	1	2	2	2	2	
6	3	6	0	6	6	
3	1	3	3	3	3	
0	----	----	6	----	----	
24	12	24	12	24	24	
2	½	2	2	2	2	
1	½	1	1	1	1	
½	----	½	½	½	½	
1	½	1	1	1	1	
2	1	2	2	2	2	
2	1	2	2	2	2	
3	1	3	3	3	3	
6	----	6	6	6	0	
2	1	2	2	2	2	
2	1	2	2	2	2	
6	----	6	6	6	6	

STATIONERY—Continued.

Allowances for ship's yeomen.

Articles.	First Class. Chicago, Philadelphia, Newark, San Francisco, and Class.	Second Class. Baltimore, Charleston.	Third Class. Brooklyn, Hartford, Lancaster, Pensacola, Richmond.	Fourth Class. Boston, Atlanta, No. 7, No. 8, and Class.	Fifth Class. Galena, Juniata, Marion, Mohican, Ossipee, Quinnebaug, Swatara, Omaha.	Sixth Class. Iroquois, Kearsarge, Adams, Alliance, Essex, Enterprise, Nipsic.	Seventh Class. Yorktown, Concord, Bennington, No. 9, No. 10, No. 11, and Class.
	3 years.	3 years.	3 years.	3 years.	3 years.	3 years.	3 years.
Books, blank .... 3-quire.	3	3	3	3	3	3	3
Books, blank (requisitions for daily expenditures)	2	2	2	2	2	2	2
Books, memorandum (small)	6	6	6	6	6	6	6
Gum-elastic loops .... dozen.	6	6	6	6	6	6	6
India rubber .... pieces.	6	6	6	6	6	6	6
Inkstands, heavy glass .... number.	2	2	2	2	2	2	2
Ink, black .... pints.	6	6	6	6	6	6	6
Ink, red .... vials.	1	1	1	1	1	1	1
Mucilage .... half pints.	4	4	4	4	4	4	4
Paper, drawing (double elephant) .... sheets.	12	12	12	12	12	12	12
Paper, blotting .... sheets.	12	12	12	12	12	12	12
Paper, foolscap .... reams.	2	2	2	2	2	2	2
Paper envelopes, official .... packages.	12	12	12	12	12	12	12
Paints, water-color .... boxes.	1	1	1	1	1	1	1
Pens, steel .... gross.	2	2	2	2	2	2	2
Pen-holders, ordinary .... dozen.	2	2	2	2	2	2	2
Pencils, black lead .... do.	3	3	3	3	3	3	3
Rulers, flat, gutta-percha		2	2	2	2	2	2
Slates, porcelain	1	1	1	1	1	1	1
Tape .... pieces.	12	12	12	12	12	12	12
Scales, Fairbank's platform, 50 pounds		1	1	1	1	1	1

STATIONERY—Continued.

Allowances for ship's yeomen

Eighth Class.	Ninth Class.	Sailing Vessels.	Paddle-wheel Steamers.	Ironclads. First Class.	Ironclads. Second Class.	Remarks.
Alert, Ranger, Yantic, Petrel, and Class.	Fortune, Leyden, Mayflower, Nina, Palos, Pinta, Speedwell, Standish, Triana, Intrepid, Alarm, Despatch, Vesuvius.	Constellation, Portsmouth, Jamestown.	Monocacy, Talapoosa, Michigan.	Amphitrite, Dictator, Miantonomoh, Monadnock, Puritan, Roanoke, Terror, Maine, Texas.	Ajax, Camanche, Catskill, Canonicus, Jason, Lehigh, Mahopac, Manhattan, Montauk, Nahant, Nantucket, Passaic, Wyandotte.	
3 years.	3 years.	3 years.	3 years.	3 years.	3 years.	
3	1	3	2	2	2	
2	....	2	1	2	2	
6	3	6	3	4	4	
6	....	6	6	6	6	
6	6	6	6	6	6	
2	1	2	2	2	2	
6	3	6	4	6	6	
1	....	1	1	1	1	
4	2	4	4	4	4	
12	....	12	12	12	12	
12	6	12	12	12	12	
2	1	2	2	2	2	One-third to be regulation paper.
12	6	12	12	12	12	To be of *three sizes*.
1	....	1	1	1	1	
2	1	2	2	2	2	
2	1	2	2	2	2	
3	1	3	3	3	3	
2	1	2	2	2	2	
1	....	1	1	1	1	
12	....	12	12	12	12	
1	1	1	1	1	1	

1. Mess and state-room furniture for commanding officers of fleets, squadrons, and vessels; state-room furniture for other officers; furniture for apartments of vessels, and mess and cooking-utensils will be supplied by the Bureau of Equipment and Recruiting, as specified in the annexed list.

2. These outfits of cabin and state-room furniture, china, etc., will be furnished only to cruising vessels. It is considered that the supply is sufficient for a cruise of three years, and no article shall be replaced or renewed at the expense of the Government during that period on any contingency whatever.

3. Articles of china, including state-room crockery, will be designated by a monogram in gold for commanding officers of squadrons, and by a monogram in blue for commanding officers of vessels. State-room crockery for other officers will not be marked. All plated ware will be marked with a monogram, U. S. N.

4. Each set of china, glass, and plated ware furnished to commanders-in-chief and commanders of vessels will be packed in suitable packing-cases, and marked with the distinguishing number of the set contained therein. Each article of the set will be also marked with the same number. In future each set will be known by its number. At the expiration of a three years' cruise each set will be returned to navy yard, New York, where it will be surveyed, the missing articles supplied, and the set made ready for re-issue.

5. All mattresses will be marked for the state-rooms for which they are intended, and with their weight, locality, and date of manufacture. Carpets are to be procured in strict accordance as to quality with the standard samples. The prices fixed are per running yard, including all expenses of making, laying, and furnishing lining, as well as loss in matching. Care is to be exercised to ascertain the actual number of running yards necessary to be used. No pattern is to be selected for apartments other than those of commanding officers of fleets or squadrons requiring more thán three-fourths of a yard to match, and for these apartments the pattern is to be no longer than will compare with the size of the cabin. All carpets for cabins are to be fitted so as to be taken up with ease. The lining should be caught together with twine, and a cover of old canvas is to be furnished for each carpet.

6. Carpets must be taken up at sea. Carpets must be covered with canvas covers whenever any work is going on liable to soil or injure them.

7. Curtains for stern and side windows, except where such windows are fitted with Venetian blinds, are to be made in halves, without trimming; each half the full width of the stuff, and not exceeding 1⅝ yards in length, lined with "silesia," gathered to the necessary fullness at the top on stout tape, and to have rings every three inches to slide on rods of brass one-fourth inch in diameter, or on hooks under cornices when those are furnished by the Bureau of Construction and Repair; to "loop up" at the side, with loop of proper material, to curtain-hooks or knobs.

8. Table-covers of woolen cloth, one for each table in each cabin, and one for the ward-room, will be allowed. An additional one of cotton-felt cloth will be allowed for each commanding officer and each ward-room. One of Turkey-red will be allowed for steerage and warrant officers, not exceeding two yards in length. The price to cover trimming.

9. Rugs, two for each cabin, and one for each stateroom in ward-room and steerage country, will be allowed.

Allowances of mess and state-room furniture.

ARTICLES.	Commanders of squadrons.	Commanders of vessels.
	No.	No.
PLATED WARE.		
Waiters	1	1
Sugar-bowls	2	2
Cream-pitchers	1	1
Castors (small, 4 bottles)	1	1
Butter-dishes	2	2
Baking-dishes (round)	2	1
Baking-dishes (oval)	2	1
Vegetable-dishes	2	2
Fruit-stands	1	1
Ice-pitchers	1	1
Spoons, table	12	12
Spoons, gravy	1	1
Spoons, salt	4	4
Spoons, mustard	1	1
Spoons, dessert	12	12
Spoons, coffee, small	12	12
Spoons, tea	12	12
Spoons, sugar	2	2
Forks, table	18	12
Forks, dessert	18	12
Forks, oyster	18	12
Ladles, gravy	2	2
Ladles, soup	1	1
Sugar-tongs	2	2
Fish-slices	1	1
Butter-knives	2	2
Crumb-scrapers	1	1
Nut-cracks	6	6
Nut-picks	12	12
Knives, carving	2	2
Knives, carving (small)	2	2
Knives, table	12	12
Knives, table (small)	12	12
Forks, pickle	2	2
Forks, carving	2	2
Tea-pots	1	1
Forks, carving (small)	2	2
Coffee-pots (Biggin, 2 quarts)	1	1

Allowances of mess and state-room furniture—Continued.

ARTICLES.	Commanders of squadrons.	Commanders of vessels.
	No.	No.
PLATED WARE—Continued.		
Soup-tureens, 4 quarts	1	1
Baking-dish linings	2	2
Cheese-scoops	1	1
Steels	1	1
CHINA-WARE.		
Sauce-boats and stands	2	2
Gravy-boats and stands (covered)	2	2
Salad-bowls	2	2
Compotiers (large)	2	2
Cups and saucers, breakfast	12	12
Cups and saucers, tea	12	12
Cups and saucers, after dinner	12	12
Cups, egg	12	12
Dishes, oval, meat, 18 inches	1	1
Dishes, oval, meat, 16 inches	1	1
Dishes, oval, meat, 14 inches	1	1
Dishes, oval, meat, 12 inches	2	2
Dishes, oval, meat, 10 inches	2	2
Dishes, vegetable, sunken knob (round)	2	2
Pitchers, 3 pints	2	2
Plates, breakfast, 8 inches	18	18
Plates, dinner, 9 inches	24	24
Plates, soup, 9 inches	12	12
Plates, dessert, 7 inches	12	12
Plates, small, deep, 6 inches	12	12
Plates, bread, 12 inches	2	2
Plates, muffin and cover	2	2
Plates, butter	12	12
Fruit-baskets	2	2
Well-dishes, 20 inches	1	1
Well-dishes, 18 inches	1	1
Ice-bowls	1	1
Pickle-shells	4	2
GLASS-WARE.		
Decanters, 1-quart	3	2
Decanters, 1-pint	3	2
Glasses, sherry	18	12
Glasses, claret	18	12

Allowances of mess and state-room furniture—Continued.

ARTICLES.	Commanders of squadrons.	Commanders of vessels.
	No.	No.
Glasses, champagne	18	12
Glasses, Madeira	18	12
GLASS-WARE—Continued.		
Glasses, finger	18	12
Tumblers	18	18
Salt-cellars (large)	4	2
Preserve-dishes	6	4
Celery-glasses	2	2
Goblets, half pint	18	12

Allowance of mess and state-room furniture—Continued.

State-room Crockery, etc.	Commander of Squadron.	Commander of Single Vessel.	Wardroom.	Steerage.	Warrant Officers.
	No.	No.	No.	No.	No.
Wash-stand basin, 16 inches	1	1	1	1	1
Water-ewers, 1-gallon	1	1	1	1	1
Brush-trays	1	1	1	1	1
Soap-trays	1	1	1	1	1
Foot-tubs (double tin)	1	1	1	1	1
Slop-jars (earthen)	1	1	1	1	1
Mattresses	1	1	1	*	1
Pillows	1	1	1	*	1
Mirrors	1	1	1	1	------
Carpet for cabin	1	1	------	------	------
Rugs for each state-room	1	1	------	------	------
Oil-cloth, or linoleum	------	------	1	------	------
Curtain material (bulkheads and ports)†	------	------	------	------	------
Curtain material (doors)‡	------	------	------	------	------
Table-covers (woolen)	2	2	1	1	1
Table-covers (cotton felt)	1	1	1	------	------
Candle-stands	1	1	1	2	1
Candle-stands (swinging)	1	1	1	2	1
Dust-pans	2	2	2	2	2
Dust-brushes	1	1	1	1	1
Water-filters	1	1	1	1	1
Looking-glass for each state-room and bath-room	1	1	1	------	1
Cover for carpet	1	1	------	------	------
Hand-bell for table	1	1	------	------	------
Bell-pulls	2	1	------	------	
Dish-covers, 18 inches	1	1	1	------	------
Dish-covers, 16 inches	1	1	1	------	------
Dish-covers, 12 inches	1	1	1	1	1
Cuspidors	2	2	2	1	1
Feather dusters	1	1	1	------	------
Chamois skins	2	2	2	1	1
Wine cloth	1	1	1	------	------
Plate-powder ... packages	12	12	4	4	------

* Each bunk in steerage, one mattress and one pillow.
† Not allowed where there are Venetian blinds.
‡ Cost not to exceed $2.50 per linear yard.

Note.—Wardroom and warrant officers' rooms, 1 set each; each steerage, 1 set.

Hereafter, in purchasing carpets or curtains in open market under the cognizance of this Bureau, the following prices per yard will be the maximum allowed:

Carpets, per yard, including making and laying, $1.35.

Curtains, per yard, for doorways and ports, including making and fitting—

For commanders-in-chief	$2.50.	Rugs	$8.00 each.
For commanding officers	2.25.	"	6.00 "
For other officers	2.00.	"	4.00 "
For bulkheads, or to cover lattice-work, air-ports, or bunks	1.75.		

○

www.ingramcontent.com/pod-product-compliance
Lightning Source LLC
Chambersburg PA
CBHW031609110426
42742CB00037B/1354

9783337723644